I Have an App Idea

INDIGORIVER
PUBLISHING

The Essential Guide to Building an App Without Tech Skills

AMANDA SPANN

I Have an App Idea: The Essential Guide to Building an App Without Tech Skills

Library of Congress Control Number: 2025909410
ISBN: 978-1-964686-57-8 (paperback) 978-1-964686-58-5 (ebook)

Editors: Linda Dessau, Juliann Barbato
Cover and Interior Design: Emma Elzinga, Hizkia Lembong, Ramish Uddin
Printed in the United States of America

First Edition

3 West Garden Street, Ste. 718
Pensacola, FL 32502
www.indigoriverpublishing.com

Ordering Information:

Quantity sales: Special discounts are available on quantity purchases by corporations, associations, and others. For details, contact the publisher at the address above.

Orders by US trade bookstores and wholesalers: Please contact the publisher at the address above.

This book is dedicated to all the dreamers who became doers,

the self-starters, and those who are committed to making it happen.

I see you. You are worthy. Your ideas have power. I can't wait to see them take form.

Thank you to my family—Dad, Mom, Dee, and Mira.

Being a part of our unit is a blessing. I could not have asked for a greater gift.

And last but not least to my community of friends, colleagues, and counterparts who supported, contributed, and offered guidance in the production of this project. Thank you for believing in my vision. I am eternally grateful.

TABLE OF CONTENTS

INTRODUCTION

Prepare to Build

I'm a publicist by trade.

I didn't go to school to be a developer.

I'm honestly not sure I've ever written a full line of code in my life. Well, outside of Myspace. *Shout-out to Tom!*

Yet, I've created and turned a profit from apps that have been downloaded by thousands of people around the world, and I believe that you can too.

It's important for me to be transparent about who I am and why I'm doing this. I'm not here to sell you on some shoddy guarantee that you'll become an app store millionaire overnight or to give you some sleazy magic bean upsell.

I am at my core an entrepreneur who happens to be passionate about helping people actualize their ideas. I graduated from college at the height of the Great Recession and didn't have the money or the resources to build the brick-and-mortar business of my dreams. So I turned to apps because I believed that even if I didn't know a thing about building them, they were the quickest and most affordable and accessible means for me to become an entrepreneur. I still believe this now.

I wrote this book because I get a constant stream of emails and letters from people who have app ideas but have no clue where to start, or who have taken the leap to start building an app themselves but are running into some costly challenges that could have likely been avoided if they would have had some insight into what to expect before they got started. *I Have an App Idea* is my "reply all."

I've spent a ton of time and a *whole lot of money learning the hard way. If I can be a catalyst to helping you achieve your app dreams quicker and with fewer Ls than I did, then I'm happy to help.*

What to Expect

This book is a step-by-step project management guide to contracting the development of an app.

It aims to provide you with an overview of what you can anticipate at every phase of the process so you can save time and money, build with confidence, and reduce the likelihood of being taken advantage of as a newcomer to the start-up space.

Though the technologies discussed in this book are ever evolving and inevitably subject to change, the concepts outlined here will give you a foundational framework for building now or in the future.

What It's Not

This is not a book to teach you how to code an app yourself or become an instant internet tycoon. That's simply not my ministry.

Who Will This Book Be Helpful For?

The following people will find this book useful:

- Anyone who has an app idea they'd like to pursue but isn't interested in coding it themselves
- Aspiring and existing entrepreneurs who'd like to build, grow, or expand their businesses with apps
- People who would like to use apps as a means of flexing their creative muscle and possibly creating a new stream of income

Sound like you? Perfect, let's get started.

How to Use This Book

1. *Read each chapter in order.* Each chapter builds upon the previous chapters to provide you with a step-by-step execution guide. Along with the text itself, be mindful not to skip any of the expert excerpts and testimonials, as they are a mini masterclass of firsthand experiences and insights from seasoned developers, designers, founders, and investors.
2. *Complete each of the activities and worksheets.* Yes, you have homework. But this isn't just mindless busywork; each of these activities has been curated to not only help you navigate each phase of the journey but also to help you start thinking strategically about building an app-based brand.
3. *Utilize the chapter checklists.* I've outlined key takeaways and work to be done from each section. Show up for yourself by meeting each milestone and checking off every box.

4. *Join our online community.* Building your app will be an exciting adventure filled with both opportunities and challenges—but you don't have to navigate them alone. Sign up for our app support group, The App Accelerator, to unlock access to exclusive trainings, tutorials, success guides, and a wealth of invaluable resources designed to support you every step of the way.

   Billionaire philanthropist and Vista Equity Partners Founder, Chairman and CEO Robert F. Smith captures the essence of what makes this community special: *"The App Accelerator is more than a resource—it's a bridge to opportunity."*[1]

IHaveAnAppIdea.net

Visit the link or scan the code to connect with like-minded innovators and bring your app idea to life. As we begin, a Steve Jobs quote comes to mind: "Life can be much broader once you discover one simple fact, and that is everything around you that you call life was made up by people that were no smarter than you. And you can change it, you can influence it, you can build your own things that other people can use."[2]

Remember, every app started as just an idea, likely from someone whose background or circumstances were not much different from your own. We all must start from somewhere, and if they could do it, why not you?

CHAPTER 1

Before You Begin

When you have big app dreams but don't have the know-how or experience to act on them, you can easily find yourself paralyzed with uncertainty. That's why when working with aspiring app founders, I always make it a point to address the need to know first—those frequently asked questions that when answered give you the gusto to get started. The sooner you can assess what you're getting into, the faster you can start making your mark.

How Do I Protect My App Idea?

Let me guess. You haven't started working on your idea because you're afraid someone will steal it? Rest assured: There are precautionary measures you could take, but none of them are entirely foolproof.

Know that even if someone dares to replicate your idea, it doesn't mean they're capable of executing it, so don't let this stop you from starting. Here are a few initial tactics you could explore to protect your idea:

- *Non-disclosure agreement (NDA):* a contract between two or more parties that outlines confidential material or information to be shared while restricting access and ensuring confidentiality. *Noncompete clause:* A clause under which one party (usually an employee or contractor) agrees not to enter into, work for, or start a similar business in competition against another party (usually the employer or client).

Developers are often willing to sign an NDA, but they may be more hesitant to sign a noncompete, depending on the nature of their business and the capacities they work within. For example, if you're hiring a developer to build your streaming app, and this developer specializes in streaming apps, signing a noncompete might impede their ability to work on other projects and make a living.

Like developers, investors also tend to be resistant to signing these documents. Consider that the nature of their work may involve a weekly analysis of dozens of companies, many of which may be similar to yours. If even a fraction of these companies required signed agreements for review, it would not only impede their ability to do their jobs but also eat up a considerable portion of their time.

- *Patents, copyright, and trademarks:* These are each forms of intellectual property that give the owner or creator the legal right to exclude others from making, using, selling, or importing a product, image, or name for a period of time.

These protections cost time and money to file, often with a review process of a few months or longer. Also, in order to get approved, you often have to prove that you are using a product "in commerce"—which means you actually have to be actively using or operating under the term, image, product, or solution. This is done to discourage people from filing on ideas they never plan to use for business in order to prevent other people from acting on them.

How Long Does It Take to Build an App?

The length of development will depend on the features and complexity of the app. Building a basic alarm clock app may only take a fraction of the time it takes to build a food delivery app.

On average, it can take about four to six[1] months to complete an app, and that's if and only if you're hitting all your development milestones consistently. That timeline can also be extended or shortened by the size of your team. Consider it would likely take a freelancer working part time on your app a lot longer to complete the project than a dedicated, full-time team of four.

More times than not, however, it takes much longer than those initial projected weeks. I give myself six months to a year to account for unexpected changes and challenges. Life happens—weddings, illness, and policy changes. You may even have your own development shifts: That "small" change you want to make to the app's business plan could force a change to your app's monetization strategy, potentially setting your development time back weeks.

My first app, Alchomy, took me a year and a half. My sixth, CultureCrush, took me less than two months. Much of your success depends on the time you dedicate to the project, your preparation for the process, and the clarity you have surrounding what you're building.

How Much Does It Cost to Build an App?

The matter of cost is by far the most common question I receive.

And the answer is it depends. I built TAMI, a tambourine app for my friend, for under $300, and I've also seen clients receive quotes for enterprise-level apps to the tune of hundreds of thousands of dollars. App costs, like the product delivery timeline, heavily depend on the features and functionality of the product you're building.

Think of it this way: If you're interested in building a basic app concept that isn't very feature rich and has concrete functionality that every user will experience in the same way—for example, a calculator app—you're likely going to spend significantly less money than it would cost to build an app intended for use across four different departments of an international corporate business, each of which may need to have a custom experience from the app to complete their respective work deliverables.

Another factor affecting cost would be who you plan to have build the app and how you decide to develop it. In the United States, an experienced developer may charge anywhere between $50–$150 per hour on average to build your app. However, if you outsource your development, you may be able to find a solid developer team across the world who charges as little as $18 per hour. I've worked with outstanding talent both domestically and abroad, and I've worked with teams domestically and abroad who left a lot to be desired. It's on you as an entrepreneur to do your due diligence to determine which development team is right for you. I'll be walking you through how to vet these teams later in the book.

"Okay, but Amanda, how much does it really cost?"

In my personal opinion, if you want to build a *native app*, or an app that is built specifically to operate natively on one specific platform, like iOS or Android, I would put aside a minimum of $5,000 per app. Again, depending on what you are trying to build and who builds it, your total cost could potentially be a lot *less or a lot more.*

Five thousand dollars is not a fixed number; it is the amount I personally suggest for first-time founders because it is large enough to build something tangible, but small enough that you likely won't be running the risk of financial ruin. An important point is that nearly all developers work on payment plans. So you will not be required to pay this amount in full, but instead in installments as the developers deliver on the various milestones of the project.

In the event you spend less than $5,000 on your product, you will still need to set aside money to market and manage the app. If you find that your app is projected to cost more than $5,000, consider if there is a more affordable way of building a similar solution.

Ultimately, setting your budget is up to you, but remember: If this is your *first app, it is 1,000 percent OK to start small, scale back, and roll out new features as you earn revenue. However, the bottom line is that you will likely need to invest considerable time and money to move forward.*

Should I Get an Investor for My App?

While I would never discourage a founder from pursuing funding, nothing says, "I'm committed," more than investing in your own idea. After all, if you're not willing to bet on yourself, why should anyone else?

It's important to know that fundraising is typically not an easy feat. Without completely dissecting the world of venture capital, know that most venture capitalists are hoping for a 10x return on anything they invest in. So unless you're already operating this business profitably without an app, you are likely pre-revenue and have yet to fully test and validate that your app could be a winner for a venture capital portfolio. Investors are much more motivated to invest in products generating revenue month over month, with loyal customers, proven traction, and, most importantly, a great team.

I asked Nichole Yembra, chief problem solver at The Chrysalis KO, what could make an early-stage company investment worthy to an investor like her. She replied, "The adaptability of the founding team. How receptive they are to feedback and to things that challenge their ideas. They must be willing to listen to the market and stakeholders and adapt quickly. The cohesion of the founding team is also super key. Businesses pivot, so you're really betting on this team's ability to win, no matter the direction."[2]

When asked the same question, McKeever "Mac" Conwell II, founder and managing partner of RareBreed Ventures shared, "One thing is to be a founder that successfully exited companies before and returned capital to their investors. That's a good sign, but every investor is different. At RareBreed, we have an extreme bias toward two things: The first is customer acquisition strategy. Start-ups having a unique or clearly repeatable customer acquisition strategy is really exciting for us. The second is traction, or your ability to grow as a proxy for your ability to execute. If you show me a pre-seed, early-stage company that's growing really quickly by more than 30 percent week over week or month over month, that's always going to be something that gets investors excited, because that's what we do—we invest in companies to make money. Founders also need to remember when you're raising capital at the pre-seed or early stage, a large portion of your ability to raise capital very often has more to do with your network than anything. And if you don't have a network, then it becomes all about your business, which is a higher bar to clear."[3]

Raising money for your app can quickly become a full-time job—and often a big distraction. I know raising may feel necessary when you are strapped for cash, but remember that sometimes you don't actually need to raise money; you just need a customer. Seeking funding may take away valuable time you could be using to build, grow, and market your app.

If you feel like you cannot move forward without an infusion of cash, I suggest starting with your family and friends or, alternatively, an *angel investor.* Angel investors are independent investors or high-net-worth individuals who deploy capital for investment. They tend to be more accessible than venture capitalists but are likely to write you a smaller check. Depending on how you structure the deal between you and the investor, be prepared to hear them ask for a larger percentage of your company for their contribution. The most ideal situation is finding an investor who is willing to invest on entrepreneur-friendly terms, so you can focus on leveraging their money to grow the company first and return their investment second.

Outside of traditional investors, you have the option of participating in start-up pitch competitions or applying for grants that can provide you with capital without loss of ownership.

The best time to raise money is when you don't need it. You never want to seek funding from a place of scarcity, as it will cause you to make decisions you might not have made otherwise. As much as you can, focus your time on making the best product you can and attracting customers. If you can start earning revenue and showing signs of growth, investors may start reaching out and approaching you—and you'll be in a much better position to set the terms on the table!

Is My Idea Worth Pursuing?

All ideas have value, but a concept on paper is not always as powerful in practice. My motto is "Apps are businesses." They are tools that solve problems for people, in exchange for money. If you find yourself questioning whether the problem you're tackling is truly important enough to pursue, here are a few key indicators of a promising app idea:

Existing Demand

Does your app address a problem that people will pay money to solve? Assess the magnitude of the problem and the current demand for a solution. Most people will take a solution if offered, but will they seek it out? And more importantly, will they pay for it?

When it comes to picking the right problem-solution to pursue, this common start-up analogy may help. *Is your solution a vitamin, a painkiller, or oxygen?*[4]

Vitamins are good for us, but many of us skip taking them daily. When we're hurt, a painkiller becomes a priority, and often feels essential. But after the pain subsides, so does our demand for painkillers. But we *need* oxygen every single day. You want to strive for oxygen-level solutions. And while most things can't compare to oxygen, you must ultimately discern if your potential customers will perceive your app as nice to have versus can't do without. At a minimum, your problem-solution should be at the painkiller tier and be adding ease or value to a specific, targeted group.

During the COVID-19 pandemic, video conferencing apps like Zoom and Microsoft Teams became oxygen-level solutions as remote work and virtual meetings not only rose in demand but became essential for public safety.

Competitive Advantage

Be honest with yourself. Are you uniquely qualified to solve this problem?

Have others attempted to solve this problem before? If so, why exactly did their solution succeed or fail? Perhaps you're the most qualified person to solve it (*let's hope this is the case* 🤞), or maybe there are a few things you don't know yet. The reality is that problems often come with hidden challenges that could prevent you from being successful in that space. From policy changes to supply chain bottlenecks, take some time to do the research and figure out what barriers may exist now or in the future.

Intellectual Property

What key features or benefits will your app have that others may have a hard time delivering as well as you do?

Competition is inevitable. Do you currently have the knowledge, experience, or a proprietary solution that positions you to develop the best app to solve customers' problems? If not, how do you plan to accomplish that aim? What will make you unique?

Alexa's proprietary voice recognition capabilities and seamless integration and management across multiple devices combined with Amazon's reach to over 300 million households gives Alexa an incredible edge over other virtual voice assistant apps in the market.

Financial Viability

Ask yourself if building this app and the business around it is financially feasible for you to execute. If you incur additional or unexpected fees during or after development, will you be able to withstand it?

We briefly talked about the costs of developing an app, but what about the other fees associated with running a business? Without the support of outside investment (*remember, funding is not guaranteed*), will you have the resources to back up your business model and generate enough revenue to keep your business running smoothly? It's one thing if you're just managing an app digitally, it's another if your business requires offline support like warehouses, a full staff, and an array of equipment to run the business behind the app.

Barney Spann, technology VP and partner at Carperks (acquired by TrueCar, Inc.), cited the true cost of building out a product road map when I interviewed him about the top things he wishes he would have known before launching an app. "Improvements always come up after the initial idea is formed, but after the initial funding request is made. Knowing what I know now, I would have set a contingency for additional funding, because variable items—like improvements on the initial design—[are factors] that you cannot anticipate, but you probably should have a provision for in every product buildout."[5]

Market Size

What is the size of the market that will buy your product or service?

Knowing your *market size*, or the number of potential users of your app, is a critical part of assessing whether the business is worth pursuing. You'll want to narrow in on a specific customer segment that is niche enough for you to focus your marketing efforts but large enough to ensure you will be able to meet your revenue goals on a regular basis.

The "right" market size is relative and can vary based on your industry and the price of the product you're selling. Stepping away from apps for a second, let's use yacht retailers as an example. A boat retailer may have a goal of one million dollars in revenue per year, but because the price of a yacht may be $100,000, they only need to sell around thirteen boats annually to reach their revenue goal. This means they can get away with having a much smaller market size. Only so many people can afford to buy boats, but they only need a few of these people to buy their boats to be profitable.

But apps typically don't charge anything close to what it costs to buy a yacht. Considering what you now know about market size, if you're selling your app in the app stores for, let's say, $1.99, you'll need a much larger market size to reach that same one-million-dollar revenue goal.

While yachts and apps seem like apples and oranges, the bottom line is that you will ultimately need to assess whether there are enough people in your target audience who are so excited about what you're offering that they're willing to make a purchase or better yet recurring purchases, that will, in turn, cover your business costs while still enabling you to turn a profit.

Accept that the best idea for you right now may not necessarily be the sexiest. Taking the next step often boils down to which idea will give you the best chance of success. It may not be the one you want to pursue the most, but it may be the easiest to execute within your current circumstances, the most likely to be profitable, or the one that can provide the fuel to fund your other ideas in the future.

Get started on your next big idea by completing the checklist below. In the next chapter, we will begin to refine the road map for building your app.

Chapter checklist

- [ ] Define your niche
- [ ] Identify your target audience
- [ ] Write a compelling bio
- [ ] Outline content ideas

CHAPTER 2

Developing a Winning Start-Up Idea

Now that you've spent some time thinking about whether your app idea is worth pursuing, we will begin unpacking the problem you're solving and the best way to deliver your app as a tangible solution.

This process is the first step in the app development framework I call *iD3*, a product development methodology that breaks down building an app into four distinct phases: *ideation, design, development,* and *deployment.* Let's take a quick look at what you can anticipate across each phase of the process:

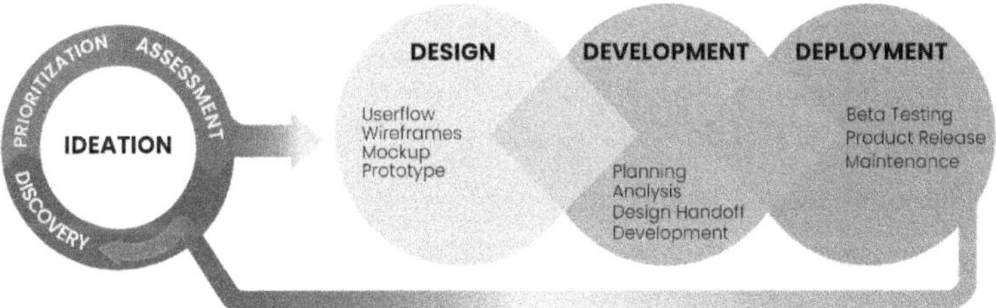

Ideation

The ideation phase centers on discovering new insights surrounding your app idea and slowly training your mind to transform that information into your product's features. You may not currently understand how the features you're envisioning can be built, but if all goes as planned you will have a developer and designer to support you with this. At this phase, your job is simply to assess the problem you're solving from different angles and generate solutions by prefixing the problem with the question "How might I?"

For instance, if the problem you're tackling is that finding the right insurance plan can feel overwhelming, the question would be, "How might I streamline the insurance search process?"

Then, begin to imagine what streamlining could look like, step-by-step, in the form of an app.

The goal is to take you from "I'd like to build an app that helps people find the best insurance plan for them" to "I'd like to build an insurance marketplace that aggregates and compares plans, prices, and coverage details from different providers."

The ideation phase is made up of three parts: *discovery, assessment,* and *prioritization.*

Discovery

At this point, you are conducting an assortment of research to understand the nature of the problem and speaking to the people it affects to get a full picture of how best to solve it. As you gain a more comprehensive view of what needs to be created and find data to support your thesis, get into the habit of logging all your potential "How might I?" solutions.

Assessment

As you take in information from your discovery process, you'll be able to develop a shortlist of ways you can deliver your solution. Take the time to think through each of their pros and cons and assess whether they are feasible, actionable, and legal to implement into your app. It's better to identify and address potential bottlenecks now rather than later.

Prioritization

Based on the research you've discovered and now assessed, you will then filter your ideas and pursue the elements that will most efficiently support your hypothesis—and this part is essential—keeping in mind your circumstances and budget.

Design

Part 2 of iD3 is the design phase. It surrounds organizing the data collected during the ideation stage and converting it into a list of visuals and product requirements—a list of features, functions, and behaviors your app needs to be efficient and effective. These requirements are used to render a prototype, or an interactive mockup that mimics your app's functionality and design but does not contain any working code.

Development

Next comes development. During the development phase, developers start producing the app. They will engineer the architecture, systems, and software to convert the prototype from the design phase into a minimum viable product (MVP),[1] or an initial iteration of your app that has just enough features to be usable for early users, who can then provide feedback. The project will be executed across milestones to ensure organization and the delivery of all integral parts.

Deployment

Lastly, the deployment phase involves performing internal and external quality assurance tests to ensure the app is stable, user-friendly, and secure. The tests seek to pinpoint weaknesses, technical errors, or potential vulnerabilities in the app before making it available to users. This is followed by the actual release of the app and the subsequent ongoing maintenance required for the product.

As we move through phases, you'll find that the biggest hindrance or help to your app's progress will likely be your preparedness and understanding of this process. That's why we'll spend the next few chapters on pre-development readiness. The more you understand your market, your customers, and the product you are building upfront, the greater your chances at success and the lower the likelihood of costly hiccups during the development process.

That said, creating a good app starts with solving a great problem.

The Problem Statement

Let's define the problem you are solving by completing a problem statement. A well-written problem statement clearly describes the issues your app seeks to solve for a user.

A good problem statement will be composed of four key components:

1. Persona: A fictional representative of your customer
2. Task: The objective they are trying to accomplish
3. Obstacle: The problem standing in their way
4. Negative Feeling: The sentiments they have about frequently encountering the problem

Imagine for a second who your app will best serve. This person feels compelled to use your app every day and even advocate its benefits to others by explaining how it makes their life better. Who is this person? Where do they live? What do they do? Are they married? Single? This imaginary figure is your *persona*.

Your task now is to identify who this person is and learn as much as you can about them.

The first app I created years ago was Alchomy, a bar locator and drink recipe app. I'm an avid traveler and when I get off the plane in a new city or country, I am often clueless about where to find a good drink. At the time I developed Alchomy, Google and Yelp could only offer me limited recommendations, such as hotel bars or chain restaurants, but I wanted to find things off the grid and under the radar that would bring a new sense of drink discovery to my trips. So I created an app for people like me.

Take a look at some of the personas I initially identified for the app.

The first personas for Alchomy

The app quickly went from a hot spot for the best bars to an all-encompassing cocktail oasis. I had a little something for everyone and found myself constantly scrambling to add new features by the day. And looking back on it, I was doing entirely too much.

My first stab at building apps was a cornucopia of doing too many things at the same time for too many audiences, which led to the app being inadequate for all of them.

Instead of focusing on just one persona for launch, I busted my budget trying to market to each of these segments of people and built features to impress them without any form of validation that they actually wanted them. In hindsight, I realize if I would have focused on making the app the No. 1 place for spirit chasers, or travelers with an interest in cocktails, the other personas may have organically found the app by user referral or our dominance in the market.

Depending on the nature of your app, you may have more than one persona, but for the purpose of not spreading yourself too thin it really behooves you to just focus on one for the product release. As your app grows and yields new areas of opportunity, you can revisit these other personas and build features to cater to them if necessary.

Use the following guide to begin crafting your persona. Jot down notes on who they are, where they live, their goals, motivations, challenges, and how your app could make their life easier.

If possible, reach out to some people within this group to learn more about who they are and how they view the world in relation to your problem. I find it really helpful to get quotes from them, or even their objections to solutions, so you best understand how their minds work.

Once you've narrowed down your persona, the next part of the problem statement is a *task*. The task is the objective your persona is trying to accomplish that the *obstacle is standing in the way of. Experiencing the obstacle is resulting in a negative feeling.*

When we compose all four parts together it will read along the lines of *a persona who is attempting to accomplish an objective but is experiencing a challenge feels* [insert negative feeling].

APP PERSONAS GUIDE

NAME:

AGE:
RELATIONSHIP STATUS:
EDUCATION:
JOB:
LOCATION:
INCOME:

PERSONALITY DESCRIPTION:

BID:

GOALS:

MAIN POINTS:

FEATURES:

BENEFITS:

QUOTES:

OBJECTIONS:

MARKETING CHANNELS:

Persona Guides can be used to log and track data on your audience, their needs and interests.

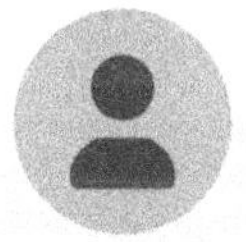

A PROBLEM STATEMENT

A [persona who feels [negative feeling] when [task, step, or objective] as a result of [obstacle].

Use this template as a guide for crafting your problem statement.

Using Alchomy as an example again, my persona would be spirit chasers or travelers with an interest in cultural cocktails. The objective would be finding cool hot spots to drink around the world. The negative feeling would be a commercialized, inauthentic food tourism experience.

If I hadn't gone too wide, my initial problem statement may have looked like this.

PROBLEM STATEMENT

For cocktail enthusiasts who want to discover amazing new drinks and the best places to have them.

Alchomy App's problem statement

For culturally curious travelers, i.e., spirit chasers, seeking authentic cocktail hotspots, the prevalence of overly commercialized and inauthentic experiences leaves them feeling disappointed and disconnected from the local drinking culture they long to explore.

Take a stab at your problem statement in the box below.

A [persona who feels [negative feeling] when [task,step, or objective] as a result of [obstacle].

____

____

____

____

____

____

Fill in the blank with your problem statement.

The Positioning Statement

You've identified the problem, now let's define your position—or how you'll solve the problem differently and distinguish yourself from any other apps or potential competitors.

Similar to the problem statement, you will also need to create a positioning statement that highlights the service your app provides and the benefits your persona will receive from it. Use the template below to write a positioning statement for your app idea.

POSITIONING STATEMENT

To [Your Target Persona], [Your App] is the [Service you Provide] that [Unique Value You Add] because [List Benefits]

App positioning statement template

Here's a real-world example: *For busy, time conscious entrepreneurs, Amazon Prime is the overnight package delivery service of choice because of its speed, convenience and comprehensive package tracking system.*[2]

Now detail in the box below how your app will solve its problem for your target persona differently from any other solution.

POSITIONING STATEMENT

To time-conscious consumer, Amazon Prime is the fast delivery service that offers unmatched variety and convenience in one
place because it provides rapid access to a wide selection of products without excessive shipping costs.

To [Your Target Persona], [Your App] is the [Service You Provide] that [Unique Value You Add] because [List Benefits].

____

____

____

____

____

____

Fill in the blank with your positioning statement.

If you're struggling to articulate your app's benefits, try a *SWOT analysis.* A SWOT analysis will break down the attributes of your app idea, the business around it, and the market you're building it in and categorize them into your strengths, weaknesses, opportunities, and threats.[3]

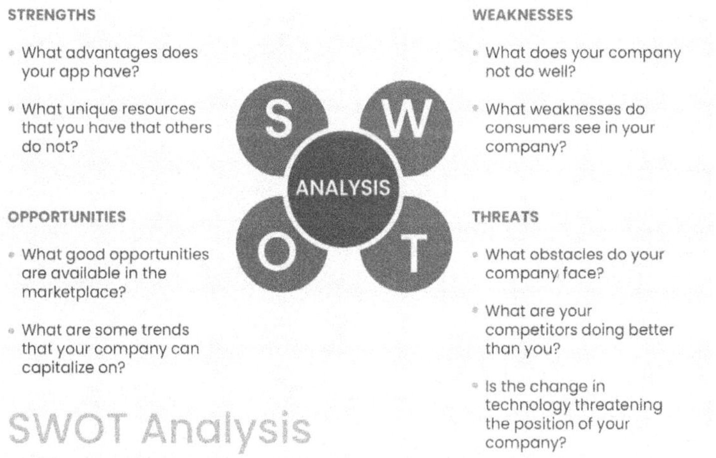

STRENGTHS

- What advantages does your app have?
- What unique resources that you have that others do not?

WEAKNESSES

- What does your company not do well?
- What weaknesses do consumers see in your company?

S W ANALYSIS O T

OPPORTUNITIES

- What good opportunities are available in the marketplace?
- What are some trends that your company can capitalize on?

THREATS

- What obstacles do your company face?
- What are your competitors doing better than you?
- Is the change in technology threatening the position of your company?

SWOT Analysis

Use the SWOT analysis chart to brainstorm unique attributes surrounding your app concept.

A strength might be your ten years' experience in the market. A weakness might be your lack of marketing funds. You might find opportunity in great partnerships you've fostered over the years that can help you spread the word about your app, but you might be threatened by changes in government policies surrounding the industry.

Writing down a few bullets for each will help you best identify where you sit in the market and help you think how exactly you can play up your advantages to make your app an attractive option for users.

Use the space below to begin identifying your app's strengths, weaknesses, opportunities, and threats.

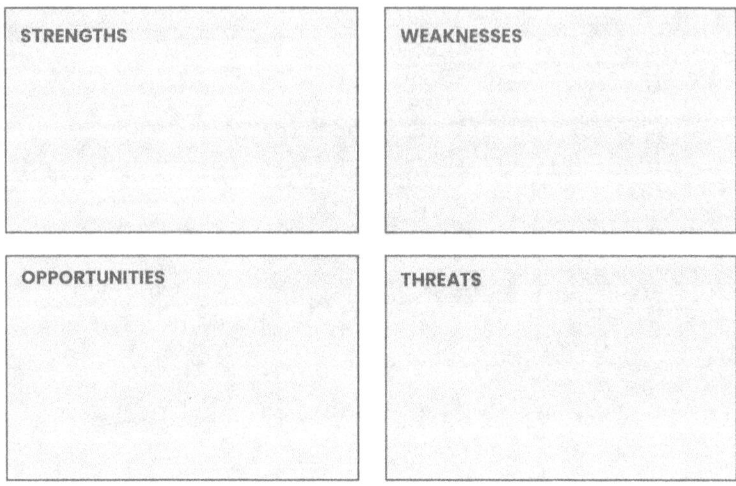

Fill in each section of your SWOT Analysis.

Product-Market Fit

Now that you have a better idea of your persona and the benefits you hope to provide to them, we can start thinking about the dynamics of product-market fit. Think of product-market fit as the practice of finding the right formula to sell the right service (your app) to the right people (your persona) at the right time.

Many appreneurs never achieve product-market fit because they either spread themselves too thin attempting to serve too many segments (like me with Alchomy), or they allow their personal feelings surrounding what the app should be to guide their decisions instead of letting their customers' desires and metrics tell them what the app should be. This is not to say that you as a founder shouldn't trust your gut, but along this road you'll quickly realize that you may often have to forgo your own feelings for what the data show will actually be successful.

Investor, philanthropist, and tech executive Nneka Ukpai shares this sentiment: "Have a bias for execution on your good ideas, but remain willing to disprove your assumptions. Founders often build what they believe their target customer wants. It's imperative to listen to the market and be willing to let go of ideas that are not supported by the market. Solicit feedback early and often, and remember that there is power in the pivot."[4]

INVESTOR INSIGHT

"Solve one big problem for one specific customer," adds Nichole Yembra. "I love the quote 'Be a painkiller and not a vitamin.' You don't have to solve this big, gigantic thing at the first go. Have your core target market and get to product-market fit with them. Then you can start expanding user and product groups."[5]

What Does Product-Market Fit Look Like?

A good sign of product-market fit is when customers are buying products as fast as you can provide them, or usage is growing as fast as you can possibly manage it. Ideally, your revenue is increasing and your customers have become walking billboards, spreading the word on your brands' behalf.[6]

How Do I Achieve Product-Market Fit?

The first step to achieving product-market fit is conducting research and customer discovery. It should be your mission to learn all you can about your industry, your prospective customers, and market trends.

APPRENEUR INSIGHT

On what he wished he knew before building a product . . .

"I would've spent more time talking to my potential customers before building anything. Don't waste time or money building anything unless you have users and customers lined up to give you their money. There are many ways to receive feedback and guidance—surveys, interviews, and no-code options with less functionality. Explore all these options to try to get pre-sales or contracts with upfront deposits. That's when you truly know someone will pay for your product. The faster you find that out, the higher your chances for success."[7]

~Eric Sonnier, Executive Director, UVI RTPark

Many of these insights can be collected by way of primary research (self-conducted research like a focus group) or secondary research (public studies and reports gathered and organized by others). The most powerful data you can possess, however, is evidence-based insights—tangible proof that customers want your app—and that's where *lean market validation* tests come in.

Lean Market Validation

Lean market validation is the process of determining whether your app is of interest to a target market. It involves conducting lean tests or experiments before building your product to ensure that users want it and are willing to pay for it. When properly implemented, validation tests can help you to reduce risk, optimize your development speed, and, you guessed it, increase the likelihood of achieving product-market fit.[8]

As you begin to navigate the start-up space, you will hear the word *lean* used quite a bit. It is typically a reference to the *lean start-up methodology* popularized by entrepreneur and author Eric Reis.[9] *The methodology advocates for entrepreneurs investigating, testing, and iterating as they build so they can rapidly discover if their business model is viable or not. You'll use these findings to build your MVP* (minimum viable product). Again, this is a version of your app with just enough features to attract and be usable by early adopters who can then validate your product idea and provide feedback for future development.

When conducting a lean validation test, you are striving to find tangible proof and reliable data to support the claim that your app idea meets the following criteria:

- *Desirable*: How can the demand for the app be converted into sales?

- *Effective*: Does the app effectively solve the problem in a way that users would be willing to pay for?
- *Viable*: Is the business model sustainable?

Some of the more commonly conducted lean validation tests include the following:

CONCIERGE MVP

The concierge MVP strategy involves manually offering the service your app would provide.

For example, let's say you want to create an app that offers on-demand mobile mechanic services. To validate your idea using the concierge method, you might put up flyers around town offering on-site car repair services. When people call to report vehicle issues, you travel to their location, make the repairs, and then collect feedback on whether they would prefer a more automated service in the future.

FAKE DOOR TEST

Using the fake door testing method, you would validate your app idea by creating a promotion for the product, even though it may not actually exist yet. A true embodiment of "fake it till you make it," conducting a fake door test involves creating only what is absolutely necessary, like a landing page website or even a graphic photo to put in a Facebook ad, to advertise the product to real potential users. This approach allows you to quickly validate interest without spending money to fully develop your app.[10]

Electric car company Tesla implemented a fake door test with their first car release, their pretotype the Lotus Elise.[11] To validate their audiences' willingness to pay, Tesla asked eager customers to put down a $5,000 deposit to secure a build date, although production hadn't even begun!

SURVEYS AND QUESTIONNAIRES

Surveys are a simple but often overlooked method for validating an app. People often love sharing their feedback, especially if a reward or perk is attached. If you have access to your market, create a brief survey and ask them open-ended questions about the problem and how they're solving it now. People will often reveal much more than you think.

Use the following blank space to write down what you discovered after you conducted your experiments.

VALIDATION INSIGHTS

Share validation insights from your experiment.

Anything surprising? Did this prove your hypothesis? Be receptive to the insights the tests provide and prepare yourself to pass or pivot on elements of your app that are not to customers' liking.

APPRENEUR INSIGHT

"The most valuable feedback you can receive is from users. It will be truthful, sometimes harsh, and honest. But it will help shape your product in more meaningful ways."[12]

~Matthew Hall, Sports Investor and Entrepreneur

If none of these experiments were a great fit for your idea, you can find more lean validation test examples and research support within The App Accelerator.

Wrap up this section by completing your checklist and proceeding to the next chapter, where we'll be taking a deep dive into relevant and related app-focused research.

Chapter checklist

- [ ] Complete your problem statement.
- [ ] Complete your personas guide.
- [ ] Complete positioning statement.
- [ ] Brainstorm your SWOT analysis.
- [ ] Strategize and execute a lean validation experiment.

CHAPTER 3

Pre-App Prep: Documenting and Discovering

You may be sitting on the next million-dollar idea, but with nearly eight billion people in the world, someone has likely already thought of it . . . or possibly even built it. The good news is even if someone else is first, that doesn't necessarily mean they're the best or the right person to solve this problem—and herein lies the opportunity.

We will begin this chapter as an extension of our iD3 ideation phase, discovering and documenting key insights surrounding our app idea so we can assess how to best build, brand, and position the product for your users' consumption.

To start, we'll be looking at your app's prospective competitors. This is a critical step in your commitment to launching an app, as it helps you understand exactly what you're up against and how you can uniquely position your app to the right audience.

As you complete the following activity, view the companies and solutions you find not as enemies but as the methods your future customers currently use to solve their problem and—more importantly—as motivation to give them a better solution.

We'll start with a competitive analysis and then round out the chapter with a brand audit.

Competitive Analysis

Our app competitor analysis is divided into three activities: a store search, a sentiment deep dive, and an online overview.

To begin the assessment, open the App Store on your phone.

Part 1: App Store Competitors

Our goal in the store search is to find similar apps to your own idea. Perhaps you already know the names of your competitors, or maybe you don't quite yet know who or what is out there.

If you don't know, start your search with *keywords*—the words and phrases people type into search engines and app stores to find what they're looking for. Use the box below to brainstorm words and terms people might use when searching for a solution to the problem you're solving. For example, for CultureCrush, a dating app I co-founded for the African diaspora, keywords might include black dating, dating app, dating for marriage, or African dating.

KEYWORD BRAINSTORM

____

____

____

____

____

____

____

Brainstorm keywords related to your app. What would you type into the search box if you were looking for your app?

Once you've got your keywords, search using those words and find a few competitor apps in or around your space. You'll want to visit each of the competitor pages to look for key pieces of information about who they are, what they do differently, and finally, how competitive they are. Your underlying objective here is to identify the things they're doing right as well as the things they're getting wrong.

COMPETITOR ANALYSIS

Competitors	Competitor A	Competitor B	Competitor C	Competitor D
Category What type of app is it?				
Platforms Android, iOS, web?				
Free / Paid				
Company Background				
Revenue Model				
Target Audience				
Time on the Market				
Main Features				
Key User Benefits				
Pain Points				
Average Rating				
Customer Review Insights				

Take note of all your app store findings in the chart above. What interesting insights did you discover?

Part 2: Sentiment Search

In part 2 of the analysis, we will be staying in the app store and assessing customer sentiment through each of your competitors' review sections.

What a company says about themselves is one thing, but what customers say about them is often a much more accurate depiction of satisfaction.

Something important to understand about ratings and reviews is that they are polarizing. Typically, only the happiest and unhappiest of customers leave a company a review, which leaves you in the dark about a large portion of the clientele. Nevertheless, this practice can give you incredible insights into how people truly feel about an app—their dislikes, their desires, or even their ongoing confusions.

Go through the reviews for each competitor app and write down commonly used words or phrases. You may see words like "bad," "scam," "game changer," or even "love." Read as many as you can and take note of commonly shared sentiments See if you could use this information to refine and strengthen the features of your app.

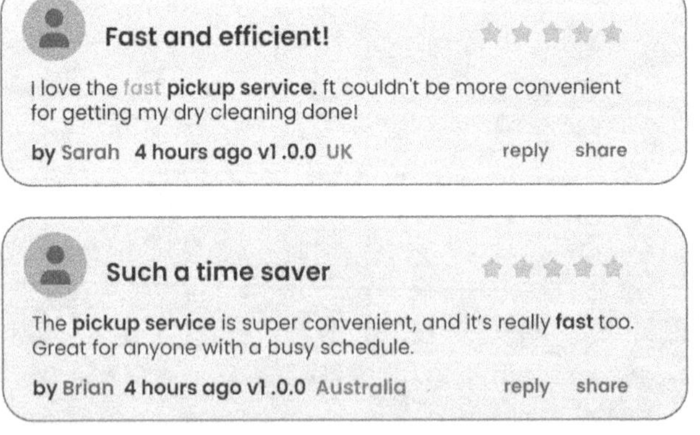

In a sentiment search, it's important to take note of recurring themes.

Use the chart below to log the words and themes you see for each competitor you uncover.

COMMONLY USED WORDS

APP COMPETITOR 1	APP COMPETITOR 2	APP COMPETITOR 3	APP COMPETITOR 4

Before we move on to part 3, let me remind you that your competition isn't always just another app. Your competitors may be existing systems or solutions that enable people to solve the problem. Before the car was invented, its competitors weren't other cars but trolleys, bicycles, and even horses. Use the box below to brainstorm competitors that aren't apps, and repeat the sentiment activity with reviews from *their Google or Yelp listings (if available).*

Part 3: Online Search

We will wrap up our analysis with the third and final leg—the multi-part online search.

For each of the competitors on your list, you'll want to identify the following:

- *Website*
- *Social media handles*
- *Content mediums: blogs, podcasts, etc. (if available)*

Once you've identified these channels, look for the following elements across all three verticals and take note of anything interesting about your competitors:

- *Brand messaging:* How clearly do they articulate what they do?
- *Aesthetic:* From the looks of their pages alone, would you trust this company with your business?
- *Recent updates:* If the last update was a few years ago, they may not still be operating.
- *Value adds:* Note if they offer supporting assets—like blogs or podcasts—to draw in or retain customers.

NON-APP COMPETITORS

COMPETITOR 1	COMPETITOR 2	COMPETITOR 3	COMPETITOR 4

How is your audience solving the problem currently? List all the ways, and note how customers are describing these solutions' pros and cons.

COMPETITORS' ONLINE PRESENCE

COMPETITOR 1	
COMPETITOR 2	
COMPETITOR 3	
COMPETITOR 4	

Use the chart to take notes on your web findings.

Brand Audit

You've taken a closer look at your competitors but now it's time for a little internal housekeeping.

At this point, many people already have a name for their app in mind (although it's perfectly fine if you don't). But absolutely nothing is worse than getting attached to a name and starting the process of creating a campaign around it . . . only to realize someone else is already using it.

You can save yourself a lot of headaches by doing a quick three-part brand audit to ensure not only that the name is available but also that there are no similarly named products or services that might overshadow your app. Follow these three steps to ensure that doesn't happen.

Step 1: Legal

Is the name legally available?

At a minimum, you need to conduct a trademark search on TESS, the U.S. trademark electronic search system, to see if the name has been trademarked.

TESS will tell you if the name is already taken and if it has any active trademarks in the business category in which you will be operating.

Should you file your trademark before you build your app? Not necessarily. As we discussed in the "need-to-knows," typically in order for a trademark to be approved, you have to be somewhat operational. The reviewer needs to see that this is a real product being used in practice to issue the mark. Otherwise, people would trademark any and every idea that comes to mind.

I learned about trademarks the hard way with our dating app CultureCrush. Few know that CultureCrush was originally named AfriDate.

Long story short, we successfully launched the app and began to grow a community around it, but when we went to file our trademark, we were denied. But why? There wasn't even another AfriDate in the App Store!

We came to find out that years prior to our filing, someone had filed a mark on the term *African Dating*. And although this person no longer had a website or app, they still had the mark. Since we were in the same product category, the reviewer thought that the names too closely resembled each other, ultimately leading to us changing our name to CultureCrush.

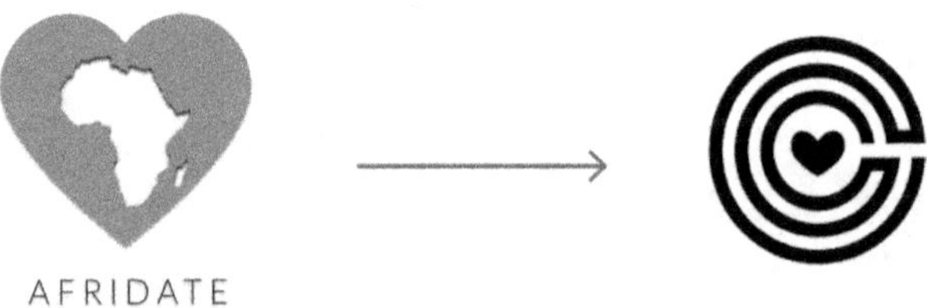

Step 2: Social

Is the handle available? How is the hashtag being used?

Search platforms like Instagram, X, and Meta to see if the handle you have in mind is available and if the hashtag is available or actively being used by another unrelated community.

For example, a quick search of the name Flare could pull up pictures of distress signals, but with a common misspelling of the name—Flair—you might see pictures of bartenders juggling bottles and doing tricks to entertain guests or even of an airline in Canada.

You want to find a name with few to no existing attachments that isn't so close in spelling to a more popular product or service that it will be hard to find when users search.

Step 3: Digital

What comes up on search engines? Is the website domain available?

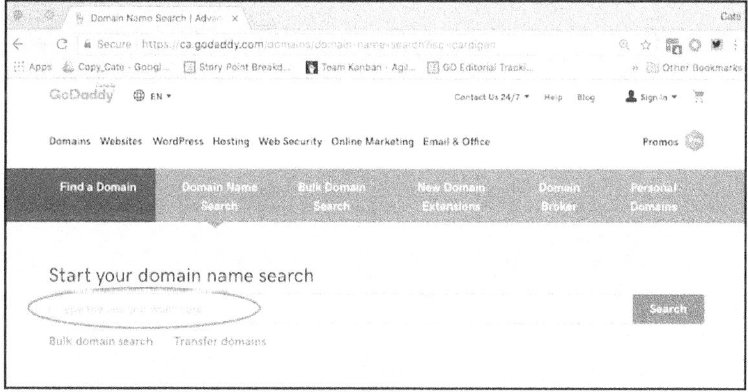

You would be surprised at how many aspiring app founders I've met who haven't ever thought to check Google Search for their idea to see if the product already exists.

Make it a best practice to not only do a search on your app idea itself but also to see what is being said about the market and if anyone is creating content surrounding the problem.

Additionally, you should visit a web host like GoDaddy and search to see if the *domain name* (the website URL) you may have in mind is available for purchase. If available, pay the annual fee to purchase your name and any similar names as soon as possible so you can begin to take ownership of your digital footprint.

In the next chapter, we'll be exploring the business models behind apps, unpacking how some of your favorite apps make money, and setting the stage for you to start making sales.

Chapter checklist

- [ ] Keyword brainstorm.
- [ ] Complete competitor analysis part 1: app store competitor search.
- [ ] Complete competitor analysis part 2: customer sentiment.
- [ ] Complete competitor analysis part 3: online search.
- [ ] Complete non-app competitor brainstorm.
- [ ] Conduct a brand audit, step 1: legal.
- [ ] Conduct a brand audit, step 2: social.
- [ ] Conduct a brand audit, step 3: digital.
- [ ] Secure domain.

CHAPTER 4

The Business of Apps

Yes, apps are a business, but the real driving force behind the multimillion-dollar industry are the distribution platforms—the app stores. Apple alone has paid out over 300 billion dollars to developers to date.[1]

There are few better feelings than receiving your monthly payout from the store, but picking the right model to enable those sales can feel like you're playing a matchmaker game.

To help you select the best path for your app, I will spend the next few pages walking you through how app stores make money and the different business models app developers and entrepreneurs have commonly used to generate revenue.

Before I start, it's important to note that this edition of *I Have an App Idea* focuses primarily on publishing an app on the Apple App Store and Google Play, but there are dozens of other app stores you have likely never heard of.

Shocker, I know; I was once as surprised as you might be. These stores are often active in countries dominated by Android or other competitor devices.

So as you begin to consider what type of app to build and how to build it, be mindful of the demographics in the places where your audience lives and which markets are prevalent in their region. Suppose your target customer is in certain parts of Southeast Asia or South America. In that case, these alternative stores may be worth exploring as an often-overlooked opportunity to own untapped markets.

Navigating the App Stores

For the time being, let's start by shifting back to the two stores at hand, starting with Apple and the Apple App Store. You will commonly hear Apple referred to as iOS or the iPhone operating system.

iOS is Apple's operating system on which all their mobile devices run; you'll need to build for it if you plan to put an app in the App Store. To get an app in the store, you'll first need to set up an *Apple Developer Account,*[2] which has the following requirements:

1. You must be at least eighteen years old.
2. If you register as an individual or sole proprietor, your name will be displayed on your public profile.
3. If you register as an organization, you'll need a *data universal numbering system (DUNS) reference number*, which you can request through a partnership with Apple.
4. You must provide banking information.

At the time of publication of this book, membership in the Apple developer program costs $99 per year.

Now let's switch gears over to Google Play. To register for a

Google Play Developer Account,[3] you simply need to complete the following steps:

1. Create or log in with a Google account.
2. Sign the Google Play Developer Distribution Agreement.
3. Pay your registration fee.
4. Complete your account details.
5. Verify your identity if required
6. Set up a Google Wallet Merchant account if you plan to sell your app or offer services for purchase within it.

To complete registration and list apps in the Play Store you must pay a onetime fee. As of my last update, this fee is $25 but may vary by region.

Visibility in these app stores provides you with access to billions of devices around the world. But please believe there's a price attached to that type of exposure, and it comes in the form of platform fees. Take a look at the fee structure of some of the most popular app platforms. **These rates and terms are subject to change at any given time.**

Apple App Store

Apple takes a 30 percent standard commission[4] on apps and in-app purchases of digital goods and services; sales of physical products, however, are exempt.

Developers who make less than one million dollars per year in App Store sales and meet Apple's qualifications are eligible to receive 15 percent commission status through Apple's App Store Small Business Program.

Payments from the App Store are distributed within forty-five days of the last day of the month in which app purchases were made.

So if you earned more than the minimum amount required to trigger a payment during August, you should see that money in your account by mid-October or sooner.

Google Play

Similar to Apple, Google previously took a 30 percent standard commission on apps and in-app purchases of digital goods and services and once again, the sale of physical products is exempt. However, in recent years, they reduced this fee to 15 percent on developers' first one million dollars in Play Store revenue. After the million-dollar threshold, the rate will again go back up to 30 percent. Orders processed through Google Play are paid out around the fifteenth of the following month.

Other popular app stores rates include the following:

Samsung Galaxy Store

Thirty percent standard commission on purchases through the app store.

Amazon Appstore

Thirty percent standard commission on apps and in-app purchases. Subscription commission is 20 percent on video apps and 30 percent on everything else.

The Amazon Appstore Small Business Accelerator Program also offers developers who make less than one million dollars per year in app store revenue the opportunity to reduce their commission to 20 percent.

Microsoft Store

To start, Microsoft takes a 15 percent commission on apps and 12 percent commission on PC games. However, that commission increases to 30 percent on all apps, games, and in-app purchases on Xbox consoles.

As you consider what type of app to build and how you'll want to structure your sales funnel, keep these fees in mind; they play a critical part in the amount you earn from month to month.

App Monetization Models

Selecting the right business model for your app starts as an art, with you making an educated guess based on the insights you've collected. Post-launch, it becomes a science, as you now have more hard data and analytics to support your sales decisions.

I've listed a few of the most popular app business models on the market below. As you review them consider these three key questions in determining which model may be the best fit for you:

1. *What service is my persona willing to pay for?* What benefit, if provided by your app, will motivate them to purchase?
2. *How much are they willing to pay for those services?* If they were to place a monetary value on this service, what would that amount be? Can they afford to spend that amount once, on a recurring basis, or at all?
3. *Is there a preferred way they'd like these services to be presented?* Based on your persona's demographics, background, and life circumstances, what is the most convenient payment method for them? What payment options are they turned off by?

Let's start with the most popular of app business models: in-app purchases.

In-App Purchases

The in-app purchases strategy involves selling physical or virtual goods within the app and earning a profit from those sales.[5] Nearly half of apps that monetize follow this model. Interestingly, only a small percentage of app users make in-app purchases, but many of the ones who do spend enough to make it a multibillion-dollar market.

With this model, you can sell a wide variety of items in an assortment of ways. Purchases can be *consumable* (items that can be bought repeatedly and spent/used at the users' discretion), or *non-consumable* (onetime payments that provide permanent access to special features, content, or functionality). For example, you could sell virtual tokens that unlock special features on different levels of a game or a onetime premium service like an ad-free app experience.

Companies that use this model: CandyCrush Saga, Duolingo, Tinder.

Virtual Goods (The Addictive Model)

A form of in-app purchase most popularly seen in mobile games, the virtual goods model enables you to sell virtual goods, or things you can't physically touch.

Let's say I launch a new app that allows users to make virtual characters or avatars. As users' attachment to their characters grows, they may want to buy their avatars clothing, shoes, a car, or even a house. Although the goods are all virtual, the money users spend on their characters is very real.

The catch: It's hard to predict which games will be a hit. There are literally millions of games on the market, but how many of them have become viral sensations on the level of Angry Birds or Pokémon Go?

Companies that use this model: The Sims, Farmville, Animal Crossing.

Freemium

The freemium model is when app entrepreneurs offer users a limited, basic, or standard version of the app for free and users then pay a fee to unlock premium or proprietary features.

Paying for an app is a large barrier to entry for a lot of people. This is why in both the App and Play Stores, over 90 percent of apps are free. This model not only gets people in the door but allows you, as the founder, to see which features customers are willing to pay for. It can also be paired with other models to give users a variety of upgrade options.

Freemium upgrades are typically executed in two ways:

1. *Onetime payments: A user pays a onetime fee to upgrade to a premium experience.*
2. *Recurring payments: A user pays monthly for ongoing access to premium features.*

The catch: With a freemium model, you will need to constantly drive new traffic to your product, as some users will never make a purchase and will stay in the freemium state forever. To make a profit, you will either need new paying customers or to add new features that freemium-level users may consider paying for.

Companies that use this model: Dropbox, CultureCrush, Canva.

Subscription

Subscription payments in apps, particularly prevalent in news, lifestyle, and entertainment categories, involve users paying a recurring fee to maintain access to a service. This model can take the form of an upfront subscription, where users pay from the start, or adopt a freemium approach. In the freemium model, users initially access content for free but can opt to pay to unlock premium features or additional content for as long as their paid subscription is active.

The catch: Most app entrepreneurs want recurring revenue, but initially it can be difficult to pinpoint where and when to place a paywall or an upsell offer in an app and what features or content to put behind it. An ill-placed paywall can quickly turn a user off from using an app.

Companies that use this model: YouTube, Pandora, Netflix.

Paid

The paid app is exactly how it sounds: not free to download. Users pay either an upfront fee to the app store or, in some cases, a recurring subscription for access to the app and the service it provides. Apps can cost anywhere between $0.99 and $999.99.

I know you must be thinking, *Who the heck is paying $900 bucks for an app?*

I've seen a number of work or utility apps deploy this model, as they know users may depend on their service on a month-to-month basis. Paying upfront becomes less of an issue when your company's livelihood depends on it.

The catch: More than 90 percent of paid apps are downloaded less than five hundred times per day.[6] To charge upfront fees for your app, you must successfully showcase its value and work to clearly articulate what differentiates you from any competitor.

Companies that use this model: TipOff—Word Guessing Game, Minecraft, Facetune.

Advertising

Imagine a billboard placed prominently inside your app. This is in-app advertising: the promotion of other companies, services, or brands on an app in exchange for a fee. Using this model enables you to offer your product for free and eases payment-related barriers to download.

There are various ways to explore advertising as an option.

The first includes partnering with an ad network that would strategically place ads on your app on your behalf. You provide the space; they source the ads and then pay you based on the metrics they set, like the number of times the ad was viewed.

The second option is creating your own advertising platform in your app, on which you could set your own rates, and brands would pay you directly instead of going through a middleman.

The catch: Securing advertisers can be a tedious and time-consuming job. Additionally, to make in-app advertising lucrative you must be able to drive a significant amount of traffic to your app on a recurring basis.

Companies that use this model: Snapchat, X, TikTok.

Affiliate Marketing

Affiliate marketing is a performance-based model in which you make referrals or drive traffic to a product or service in exchange for commission on the prospective sale of the goods or even a new lead.

Outside the app world, this is how many bloggers make their money. That blog post where *BrunchBlogHERgirl123 conveniently provides direct links to all the pieces she wore to last Sunday's brunch? All affiliate links, each with an embedded tracking code that could provide your blogging brunch babe with commission income. Now one purchase may only make her a few bucks, but if this happens dozens of times a day—someone could earn quite a pretty penny.

Affiliates typically profit in one of two ways:

1. *Cost-per-action (CPA): This is when the affiliates get a reward for an action. For example, a tech blogger may review an app and get $2 for every install that comes from their referral.*
2. *Revenue sharing: As described above, the affiliate gets a percentage of the revenue of the sales they help generate for the advertisers.*

The catch: Not only do you typically need a large amount of recurring traffic with this model, but an increasing number of laws are emerging surrounding increasing transparency and information surrounding the promotion of products.

Companies that use this model: Podcast Addict, Amazon, Honey.

The models listed here only represent a small snapshot of the ever-evolving landscape of app monetization. You don't have to limit yourself to what you've seen before; feel free to blend and modify models to find what works best for you and your customers.

When we launched CultureCrush, the app enabled users to search for eligible matches based on nationality, ethnicity, and tribe. The app employed a freemium subscription model in which users would get access to the app for free but pay a monthly fee if they wanted access to premium features. We predicted the app would be more popular in countries with large African immigrant populations and selected our business model based on their buying habits in those markets.

As the app grew, however, we began to see an overwhelming number of app downloads come from Brazil. As exciting as this was, we also noticed that the volume of our subscriptions started to dwindle. We dove into learning more about Brazilians, why our service was of interest to them, and what was the roadblock preventing them from upgrading to our premium subscription.

From our search, we interestingly found that more than half of Brazilians identified as Black or of mixed race,[7] making it an ideal market for our platform. We learned that Brazilians are big on dating apps and are even open to paying for them, however they prefer to pay in smaller "micro" payments for individual features as opposed to monthly subscriptions that provide multiple add-ons at once. With these insights, we took the necessary steps to restructure the app so they could still access the same features but in smaller, à la carte payments that felt more favorable and familiar to them in their region.

I share this story as a testament that personas occasionally evolve and sometimes they change altogether. However, their needs should always be your North Star. Dedicate time to learn more about them on an ongoing basis and structure your business model around what you find.

Reference your chapter checklist below to help you narrow down the right model for you. In the next chapter, we'll consolidate your choice while exploring key bits of information surrounding how apps are built.

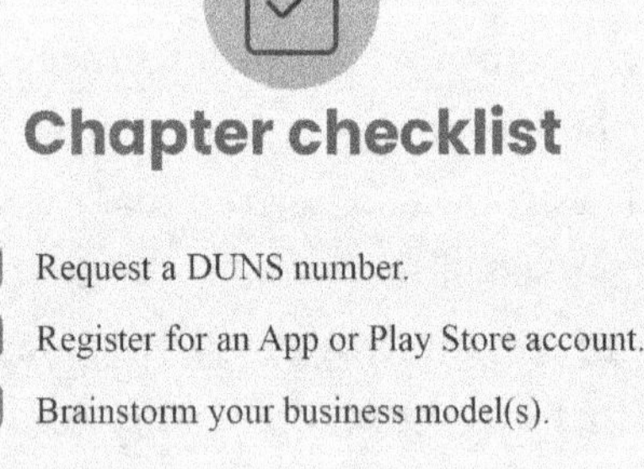

CHAPTER 5

App ABCs: Design and Development Prep

We're inching closer to the development phase of this process, but before you stake your claim as the next Zuckerberg, it's important you become familiar with some of the terminology that will inundate your world in the next few weeks.

There is no worse feeling than confidently going into a developer meeting only to be demoralized by some question or comment that went right over your head, so I find it helps if I can provide founders with a quick overview of the types of apps that exist as well as the software and solutions they are built with.

Categories of Apps

While there are dozens of different types of apps, it's commonly understood that they can be grouped into three primary categories: *native, web*, and *hybrid apps.*[1]

These groups were created and organized based on the technology used to code them.

Native Apps

Native apps are apps that were created for one specific platform or operating system.[2] Because they're built to optimize the functionalities of one platform, you can make the most of that particular device type, giving users access to device-specific features and tools like access to their contacts or their camera. For the very same reason, however, you won't be allowed to mix and match device-specific features—for example, you cannot use the native Android app you built on a Windows phone. Each device type—Apple, Android, Windows, etc.—will require its own separate app.

WHY SHOULD I BUILD A NATIVE APP?

Since native apps are designed specifically for their platforms, many people consider them advantageous because they offer a more interactive user experience that operates more quickly and intuitively.

Pros:

- Performance speed is faster because the code is specific to the device and its respective operating system (OS).
- Native apps can optimize and make use of device-specific functionalities and features, like accessing the camera on a phone.
- Designs tend to look better on native apps because they were built specifically for that device's dimensions.
- Native apps can function either online or without an internet connection.

Cons:

- Since you have to build for each device, building native apps can be more time-consuming and costly.
- Native apps often have longer product release cycles because each device must be tested separately.
- Native apps require separate code bases for each device, which you must update individually when you want to add new features.

Examples of Native Apps: Pokémon Go, Waze, Evernote.

Web Apps

A web app is software that can be accessed from a web browser on any device that has an active internet connection. Whereas native apps tend to be standalone apps built for specific operating systems that require you to download and install an app on your device, web apps are essentially websites that can adapt to assorted mobile screen and device sizes. When you install a web app, you are often just bookmarking the app on your device.

One kind of web app that you may hear mentioned on your journey is a *progressive web app* (PWA). This is an extension of a website that can be saved on a computer system or device but used like an app. This type of web app is rising in popularity as it strives to deliver an elevated level of performance, regardless of device type or network conditions.

WHY SHOULD I BUILD A WEB APP?

Web apps are not only accessible on all devices but also tend to be less costly than native apps and require less effort for updates.

Pros:

- Web apps mean reduced business costs as you are not building for specific devices.
- Web apps often have quicker installation processes.
- Web apps are easier for developers to update in real time.

Cons:

- Web apps often require an active internet connection to work.
- Developers can't always optimize device-specific features as with native apps.

Examples of Web Apps: Pinterest, Yummly Web, Asana.

Hybrid Apps

Combining the best of both worlds, hybrid apps are mobile apps built with web technologies for cross-platform compatibility—meaning they look and feel more like native apps but can be distributed across multiple app stores. These apps are best for projects that don't require high-performance functionality or full device access of one operating system or another.[3]

WHY SHOULD I BUILD A HYBRID APP?

Since a hybrid app's code is shareable across multiple operating systems, they tend to be much quicker and less costly to build. But because each operating system has their own unique design dimensions and functionalities, a hybrid app may not be able to offer as many in-app features or be as aesthetically sleek as a native app. Nevertheless, hybrid apps are still a very attractive option for getting the first iteration of your app—your MVP—on multiple app stores in a hurry.

"Wait, I don't understand! Why wouldn't hybrid apps be as attractive as a native app?"

Hybrid apps share one single bundle of code across many systems, right? Imagine your hybrid app as a 10 x 10 photo. Now try to squeeze that photo into Android's 10 x 8 frame or iOS's 7 x 9 frame. The picture will still look pretty good, but there may be some slight distortions.

Pros:

- Hybrid apps are easier and faster to build than native apps, as they can be deployed for multiple operating systems at once.
- Shareable code makes hybrid apps cheaper to develop than native apps.
- Since a hybrid app has a single code base, new features can be implemented swiftly.
- Hybrid apps work offline.

Cons:

- If your app is feature-rich with many functions it will run more slowly.
- Hybrid apps tend to be more expensive than web apps.
- Hybrid apps can be less interactive than native apps.
- Hybrid apps cannot always perform operating system–specific tasks with ease.

Examples of Hybrid Apps: TipOff—Word Guessing Game, Gmail, Evernote

Selecting your app category will be a decision you make alongside your developer. As you decide, keep in mind the pros and cons listed above as well as these key considerations:

- *Maintenance:* Hybrid and web apps tend to be easier to maintain than native apps. Do you have the technical resources or a supporting team to help you manage the app? Do you have the budget to bring on a maintenance team?
- *Storage Size:* Is data usage a key concern for consumers in your market? A smaller, leaner app might be more suitable for them. Since hybrid and web apps are composed of web components, they will not require as much storage space on a user's device.
- *Device and OS Access:* Are there device-specific features and functions you'll need for your app to work?
- *Budget:* If you're working with a smaller budget, building one app like a web or a hybrid app may be a good starting place for your MVP. You can always upgrade to a native app in time.

When it comes to apps, bigger isn't always better. Starting small and scaling gradually is often the best approach. And as you grow, understanding essential terminology will be vital for collaborating with your developers and ensuring smooth progress.

App Terms to Know

Now that we know the categories of apps, let's delve deeper into some of the most common tools and terminology used in building those apps. Even if you never write a line of code, it certainly helps to be familiar with these acronyms and phrases when and if your developer references them. And who knows? As your appreneur star rises, they could become a regular part of your vocabulary as well!

Software Development Kit (SDK)

WHAT IS IT?

An SDK is an installable collection of tools and programs for software developers that enable them to create apps for specific platforms or frameworks. SDKs are designed for specific platforms, thus you would need an iOS SDK to build an Apple app.

HOW IT'S USED

Also known as dev kits, SDKs consist of a variety of helpful resources and assets including code samples, guides, libraries, and documentation that a developer can use to develop your application, without having to write every line of code from scratch.

Android Application Package (APK)

WHAT IS IT?

An APK is an Android application package. It is a file format used to package and deliver mobile apps to Android devices.

HOW IT'S USED

When your Android app is completed, your developer will upload your APK into the Play Store.

iOS application archive (IPA)

WHAT IS IT?

An IPA is essentially the iOS equivalent of an APK; it's a file format for storing and delivering apps to iOS devices.

HOW IT'S USED

IPAs are structured in a way that the App Store will recognize and accept them. You must upload the file through the store's submission process; IPAs, unlike APKs, cannot be uploaded directly onto a user's device.

Application Programming Interface (API)

WHAT IS IT?

An API is a mechanism that uses a set of protocols to enable two software components to communicate. They work to integrate new applications with existing software systems, increasing development speed and simplifying the product maintenance process in the future.

HOW IT'S USED

Many software companies or services make their APIs available to the public for developers to build with. Let's say you'd like to add a geo-location component into your app. It may take weeks or even months for your developer to build this natively, but with the Google Maps API you could have this functionality in your app in a matter of hours. Google Maps makes its API available and sets parameters around how people can use it.

Content Management System (CMS)

WHAT IS IT?

A content management system (CMS) is like an admin panel for your app, allowing you to manage and update content without needing deep technical skills. This dashboard will enable you as the owner to make changes to text, images, and other elements without touching the app's core code.

HOW IT'S USED

Using a CMS can be a game changer for app content management, especially from a nontechnical founder's perspective. For example, when I developed my first app, Alchomy, which featured over 16,000 cocktail recipes, not having a CMS meant any content update—like altering a single recipe—required changes to the app's code. It was an absolute nightmare for someone without a technical background. A CMS simplifies this process, allowing for quick and easy updates directly through a user-friendly dashboard, avoiding the complexities of code.

Front-End Development

WHAT IS IT?

Front-end development is the development of the user interface of a website or app, the parts that users view and interact with on their devices.

HOW IT'S USED

Everything a user touches, from sign-in pages to buttons to links to on-screen animations, falls under front-end development.

Back-End Development

WHAT IS IT?

Commonly referred to as server-side development, back-end development is all the behind-the-scenes components of the app that are required to perform any action but that the users don't necessarily see. The *back end* consists of elements like databases, APIs, and servers.

HOW IT'S USED

Think about the last time you registered an account on an app. You may have typed in your name, created a username, selected a password, and maybe even uploaded a profile picture. But after you pressed the submit button, where did that information go? That data was added to a database, but you never saw it happen and that's because it was stored on the back end. The back end is the code that stores and receives requests from your users and contains the logic to send the appropriate action or information back accordingly.

Server

WHAT IS IT?

A server is a computer that is optimized to receive and process incoming requests to visit app pages and "serve" users back the pages they want to view.

HOW IT WORKS

Every time you visit a website or app, it is likely hosted by a server. The server is simply an internet-connected computer whose sole job is to serve web pages to internet or app users upon request.

Software Stacks

WHAT IS IT?

Stacks are bundles of software that compose your app. Software stacks are components and subcomponents that work together to deliver a piece of software—in this case, your app—to the end users. These components could include operating systems, protocols, databases, and more—all stacked on top of each other.

HOW IT'S USED

Software stacks play a critical role in the development of apps by providing a complete set of technologies designed to work together to build, run, and manage applications. You may hear developers referring to apps "running on" or "running on top of" these stacks.

Popular Stacks include

- LAMP (Linux, Apache, MySQL, and PHP),
- MEAN (MongoDB, Expressjs, Angularjs, and Nodejs), and
- WAMP (Windows, Apache, MySQL, and PHP).

By understanding these basic app terminologies, you'll not only be better equipped to communicate with developers but also have a firmer foundation for building products. That said, we'll wrap up this chapter with a high-level overview of the programming languages that power these stacks. This isn't about making you a software aficionado but rather about giving you some familiarity with these languages for when and if you encounter them.

Programming Languages

Now, if you don't have any tech experience, the next part can get a little scary, but I promise to try to make it as painless as possible.

Programming languages, or systems for writing computer programs, are a critical component of bringing your idea to life.

Just like thousands of human languages exist, there are numerous programming languages developers can use to communicate with a computer, each with its own distinct features and some with commonalities.

Although you may never see yourself coding, knowing the basics about programming languages keeps you in the loop with your developer and helps you better understand their decisions, suggestions, or recommendations surrounding how your app should be built.

What follows is a small sample of some of the most common coding languages used to build mobile apps.

For Android

Java

The most popular and supported language by Google, Java was regarded as the official language of Android app development for some time, and it is still one of the most popular languages represented in the Play Store. Java was initially created in 1995 and is an object-oriented language, which means it implements objects and their associated procedures and directives within context to create software programs. Outside of Android apps, it is commonly used for developing desktop applications and back-end web frameworks.

JAVA KEY FEATURES

- Can be used everywhere on the web
- Noted as being a scalable solution with an architecture and an ecosystem to support the development of both small-scale projects to large systems
- Offers a comprehensive set of APIs for various tasks, simplifying development

Python

Python is an object-oriented, high-level programming language intended for general programming as well as rapid app development. Many developers use Python to create Android apps because it is said to simplify the most complex development process and provide extremely fast mobile apps.

PYTHON KEY FEATURES

- Corporate-level business-friendly, due to its capacity for rapid development and maintainability
- Touted as being relatively easy to understand and amateur-friendly
- Supports multiple systems and platforms—it can run on Windows, macOS, and Linux, another operating system

For iOS

Objective-C

Created in 1984, Objective-C is a spin-off language that added small-talk-style messaging to another popular language, C. Apple selected this language, and it became a vital part of creating a new wave of apps that were regarded as healthier and more scalable. To this day, it is primarily used for macOS and iOS applications and operating systems.

OBJECTIVE-C KEY FEATURES

- Commonly used code, so relatively easy to find developers who utilize it
- Has a lot of legacy code, or source code inherited from someone else or inherited from an older version of the software, which gives developers a lot to work with
- As the original language for iOS devices, it has a track record of proven performance and reliability in creating high-quality apps

Swift

In 2014, Apple released Swift, a general-purpose programming language developed specifically for its different operating systems like iOS, tvOS, macOS, and watchOS. While it can be used alongside Objective-C, Swift is touted for its superior features and capacity to be easily maintained. It is also said to have eliminated many of the potential security risks found in the Objective-C language.

SWIFT KEY FEATURES

- Noted for its premium performance, Swift was designed to be fast and efficient.
- Swift is supported and promoted by Apple, essentially ensuring its integration with the latest Apple hardware and software innovations.

- The platform has a playground feature, or an interactive environment for developers to experiment, learn, and prototype code.

For Hybrid Apps

JavaScript

Arguably one of the most popular languages for mobile apps and development in general is JavaScript (not to be confused with Java). It can power an array of things like interactive images and forms or processing and payments. Some of the programming frameworks based on JavaScript include jQuery, Angular, Vue, Svelte, and React.js. The React Native framework has risen in popularity due to its ability to use the JavaScript language to create cross-platform hybrid apps that can appear on both Android and iOS.

JAVA SCRIPT KEY FEATURES

- JavaScript easily integrates into other technologies and programming languages.
- It's supported by all major web browsers, making it the standard language for web development and interactive websites.
- The language continues to evolve with frequent updates and enhancements.

Dart with Flutter

Developed by Google, Dart is an open-source programming language, which means it was made available to the public, allowing anyone to view, modify, and distribute the code. Flutter is a design toolkit on Dart. Flutter allows developers to create mobile, web, and desktop applications from a single code base. This makes it a popular choice for hybrid app development, providing a seamless user experience across different platforms.

DART WITH FLUTTER KEY FEATURES

- Has a "Hot Reload" feature that enables faster changes and development
- Single code base for multiple platforms
- Highly customizable for beautiful design interfaces

React Native

React Native is a dynamic programming framework created by Facebook, designed to empower developers to build native-style applications for both iOS and Android platforms using a single JavaScript code base. This unified approach not only boosts development efficiency but also ensures consistent high performance across both iOS and Android. It offers you a pathway to develop native-like apps without the complexity of maintaining two separate code bases.

REACT NATIVE KEY FEATURES

- React Native can help slash time and cost, since you only have to build one app that can run on both Android and iOS.
- It uses modular components that enable developers to keep the code clean and reusable.
- It includes a live reloading feature, which give developers app previews to see their code changes in real time.

See, not so bad, right? Understanding these programming languages might seem like a necessary evil, but doing so is crucial for developing your app effectively. As we conclude this chapter, we will begin to transition out of the discovery leg of our journey and ease our way into the assessment portion of ideation. Right now, determining the best way to build and deliver your app should start being top of mind. In the next chapter, I'll walk you through options to do just that.

CHAPTER 6

Your Development Options: Choosing the Best Path for You

I **know the last** section may have started to feel a little overwhelming, but don't get discouraged. You're closer than you think. Stay with me.

We've previously discussed the three primary categories of apps and how some of your favorite apps make money. Now we'll get into some methods and practical paths to bring your app business to life, as well as some real-world examples of products you may not have even realized were apps!

Alternative App Options

When we think about building apps, most people's minds default to coding a product from scratch . . . but what if we didn't have to?

App Clones

Introducing app clones, also commonly referred to as app scripts. Just like the name suggests, clone scripts are ready-made replicas of existing apps on the market. In my opinion, clones are one of the most valuable yet underutilized resources in app development.

WHY YOU SHOULD CONSIDER CLONE APPS

Nearly half the app ideas people approach me about are some iteration of an app that already exists. Tinder for medical professionals, Airbnb for dance studios—I've heard it all.

If this is the case for you, ask yourself why you would spend your time and money building something from the ground up when you can buy a license for a clone and customize elements of that clone to suit your unique needs.

Clone scripts are as follows:

- *Cost-efficient:* They allow you to focus your development efforts on making customization to the clone as opposed to building a new native or hybrid app.
- *Time-favorable:* Since the clone is typically ready for release upon purchase, you can get your product to market faster.
- *Easy to re-skin:* A re-skin is the process of giving an app a design makeover on the front end. The app will still function the same on the back end but has a fresh new look to users. Clone developers know their apps will need to be re-skinned to be published to an app store, so they build and organize their code in a way that new designs, integrations, and edits are easy to implement.

With that, understand that purchasing a clone is similar to making any other digital purchase like a course or an e-book. Clones can be found online in digital marketplaces, and a few agencies even specialize in creating them. Typically, when you purchase a clone, the developer will package it so you can buy a license for a single-time use to build one app. However, once you purchase it, that doesn't mean you will receive dedicated support. You may be on your own to find a new developer to make the changes you'd like to see integrated into the app. Sometimes, you do luck out, and the developer who sold the clone will offer re-skin customization services as an upsell alongside the purchase.

Additionally, there may be occasions when you find the perfect clone, but it's a few years old. With the rate at which technology moves, it's likely to be outdated and require more updates and customizations than new products or ones that have been updated regularly. Before you purchase a clone, check for the last update listed on the purchase page. Feel free to reach out to the developer to see if they offer re-skins for a fee.

Smart TV Apps

Within the past week, you probably caught up with one of your favorite shows on Netflix, Hulu, or Disney+. But I bet you never stopped to think that you were watching that programming through an app!

Smart TV apps are also known as OTT apps, or over-the-top applications. These apps deliver video and sometimes text-based content to your smartphone, tablet, or smart TV, as opposed to going through more traditional distribution verticals like cable. Many smart TV apps are simply Android apps that have been modified for a particular platform like Roku, Android TV, or Amazon Fire. The potential is endless here, as smart TV apps provide many entertainment options from streaming to games or even social networks.[1]

Being listed as a smart TV app is actually very similar to listing on a mobile app store. Like the App or Play store, most smart TV platforms have their own registration process as well as fees they charge for listings and purchases made within their platform.

WHY YOU SHOULD CONSIDER SMART TV APPS

Their massive reach is the primary reason for considering smart TV apps. Connected TVs and devices are in more than 700 million homes, representing well over a billion televisions or potential users for you. Many of the same popular app business models and platform fees still apply here. Imagine one million people using their television remotes to opt in to a $1.99/month subscription to your app from the comfort of their living room sofas.

KweliTV is a popular OTT app that offers diverse streaming content.

KweliTV[2] is an example of a successful smart TV app that is thriving in the market. The platform celebrates global Black culture through curated, award-winning indie films and programming. Users can subscribe to the service through their TV or online and pay a monthly fee to access an assortment of original content, movies, documentaries, and shows from independent creators across the African diaspora.

Desktop and Browser Extensions

Chrome, Safari, Firefox, Edge, and so on. They help us navigate the internet, but with the invention of browser extensions, they've begun to offer so much more.[3]

Browser extensions are small software applications that add a new capacity or functionality to a browser. You may recognize them as those little widgets typically nested in the upper-right corner of your web browser.

You download them from your browser's app store (yes, browsers have their own app stores!), and then they install right on the browser or desktop. Right now, in my Chrome browser, I have a screen recording extension, both Zoom and Skype, a keyword search tool, as well as a coupon code finder for retail sites.

WHY YOU SHOULD CONSIDER A BROWSER EXTENSION

Similar to smart TV apps, browser extensions have an incredible reach. They empower us to work in new ways and enable us to perform tasks in one window with convenience and ease.

WordPress

Sometimes you don't need an app; you just need an online presence.

Before you spend your time and money on a mobile app, ask if you could accomplish your goal with a website.

WordPress is a free content management system you can use to create a website, blog, or app. WordPress's architecture gives you the ability to upload templates and customize your site by installing plugins to add functionalities. This framework essentially gives you the freedom to create nearly anything you want—stores, galleries, forums, forms, directories, and more!

WHY SHOULD YOU CONSIDER WORDPRESS?

Not only is WordPress beginner-friendly and easy to use, it's also highly customizable—with over 55,000 plugins for you to build with—and is mobile responsive, which means that when displayed on a mobile phone, the site automatically adjusts to the device's dimensions. More than 800 million websites currently use WordPress to display their content and services.[4]

Other than WordPress, there are an assortment of website builder tools that provide quick setup and installation for a small monthly subscription fee.

Deciding How to Build

At this point you likely have a pretty firm grasp on the type of app you're leaning toward, so let's go ahead and get into how you want to build it.

This book primarily focuses on working with a development agency, but I would be doing you a disservice as a mentor and your unofficial app bestie if I didn't mention all the other ways you can make it happen. You may find that one of these options may better align with your business model or budget.

DIY: App Builders (No- or Low-Code Platforms)

App development has come a long way since its inception, and in recent years we've welcomed a wave of platforms that enable you to build apps without writing a single line of code. These platforms offer libraries of modules, widgets, and plugins that founders can drag and drop into a template, customize, and then upload to the App or Play Store.

App builders typically provide users three different options to help you create your product:

1. *Build-it-yourself:* Take the bull by the horns and start dragging and dropping your solution yourself. While there may be a learning curve, most modern platforms are relatively easy to grasp and offer an assortment of add-ons like social media plugins, geolocation widgets, e-commerce capacities, and more.
2. *Template:* This option was created for people who may have an app idea in a popular business category like a restaurant, gym, or conference. Some platforms will give you the option of using their standard templates, which they have prepped and readied with features. On these templates, you can make structural and visual changes to things like the logos, photos, or fonts and then deploy them to the App or Play stores.
3. *Done-for-you:* Sometimes founders want the convenience of a DIY tool without having to do it themselves. An increasing number of app builder platforms are beginning to create agencies within their company. These in-house teams will build your app on your behalf on the app builder platform, for an additional fee. While this option will be more expensive than building it yourself, it will still likely be less than building the app off-platform on your own and is almost guaranteed to reduce the time it takes to produce the product.

While app builders are an ideal option for building an MVP, it's important to note that they're not always great for custom solutions. Your app will likely only be able to include the modules and features offered by the platform of your choice, so please take your time selecting the right tool for you. Our online community, The App Accelerator, has resources to help you find the best no-code tool for you.

Another critical note to share about app builders is that these platforms license their software for you to build on. In exchange, you will be required to pay a monthly or annual fee to make your app continually available for use. If you stop paying, the app will no longer be visible to your users.

Partnerships for Equity

If you're looking to build a team to support your company, partnerships for equity can be a cost-saving and highly collaborative path. By taking this route, you could potentially find someone who is as invested in your project as you are and who will complement your expertise with their own unique skills.

Once you've registered your app as a business in your city, state, or country, you would work with a start-up attorney to structure your equity and issue shares to key members of the founding team based on their expertise, time commitment to the project and the milestones they agree to meet within their role.

If you do decide to issue equity to team members or a co-founder, make sure you *vest*—or distribute—that equity over a period of time. Life happens and sometimes people leave companies unexpectedly; you would not want to lose 10 percent of your company to someone who was only involved with it for three months.

Partnerships for equity can take many forms, but three of the most common development relationships include the following:

1. *Technical co-founder*: If a founder is a person who has conceptualized the idea, the co-founder is the person who joins with the founder to build and establish the business, working in tangent to make the business successful. The technical co-founder's job is to lead the development of the product; however, on some occasions, they may take on as much

responsibility as the founder. Technical co-founders receive a larger share of equity than other team members for their contributions to building the product.

2. *Chief technical officer:* With this option, your developer may not identify as a co-founder but still agrees to provide their technical expertise, usually in exchange for a mix of monetary payments or/and a smaller share of equity.
3. *Start-up studio:* Also known as a venture studio or start-up factory, start-up studios are organizations that provide both technical and nontechnical support, as well as resources, to help a company go from concept to creation. Start-up studios are typically led by established founders and usually have a goal of launching multiple companies in succession. Studios may help you to build faster, bigger, and better, but are often hard to get into and are likely to take much larger portions of equity.

Consider that equitable partnerships are kind of like a marriage. You are bound together by a product and a dream of delivering it, but these relationships can occasionally end in divorce. Not only can it be hard to find someone who shares the same passion and dedication to your app baby as you, but the stress of working for little to no money can send what would have otherwise been a healthy work relationship over the edge.

Freelancer

If you would like to retain your equity and simply pay to have your app built, consider hiring a freelance app developer. Freelance developers are self-employed coders who get paid per project in exchange for their skills and services. Since they aren't tied to an employer, freelancers set their own rates and may often be working on multiple projects at once.

Working with these specialists for hire may reduce your development costs as they are generally cheaper than a team, but please keep in mind that all developers are not created equal. You'll need to vet them ahead of time to ensure they have the experience you need, are communicative and reliable, and have the time management skills to meet your deliverables.

Development Agencies

The remainder of the book will focus on working with development agencies, or a team of people with individual specialties who collectively work together to build apps and software products.

While agencies tend to be a little more expensive, you'll reap the benefits of a small suite of experts who can not only build your product but counsel and advise you along the way. With more than one set of eyes on a project, you can build quicker and catch mistakes faster.

Like freelancers, agencies tend to work on a project-to-project basis but can be informally thought of as long-term partners for your project. A great agency is going to actively work for you and with you to maximize your product's chance at success even though they have no ownership. After all, your wins are a reflection of their development skills, so they should want you to be successful.

As we round out this chapter, we are concluding the ideation phase of your app journey. We've covered quite a bit up to this point, and if you have completed each of your chapter checklists, you should have clear thoughts on elements like the problem you're solving, its target audience, validation of your idea, and the path you'll take to develop your idea. Now you'll need to solidify them by putting them on paper.

Use the following App Business Model Canvas to document critical components of the product you're developing. This document can be used as a reference point to help you maintain clarity throughout the project and clearly articulate the product to your developers.

APP BUSINESS MODEL CANVAS

PROBLEM	SOLUTION	KEY METRICS

UNIQUE SELLING PROPOSITION

UNFAIR ADVANTAGE	MARKETING CHANNELS	CUSTOMER SEGMENTS

COST STRUCTURE

REVENUE STREAMS

Consolidate information about your app-based business in this App Business Model Canvas.

Chapter checklist

- [ ] Review alternative app options.
- [ ] Decide path to building your app.
- [ ] Complete your App Business Canvas.

CHAPTER 7

Designing Your App

You've strategized and solidified your idea, and now it's time to visually bring it to life by entering phase 2 of our framework: design.

In this chapter, I'll provide insights and prep work to help you conceptualize your app's look and feel. This involves both *user experience* (UX), focusing on overall satisfaction and usability, and *user interface (UI), addressing the visual and interactive elements. While this won't replace the expertise of a seasoned designer, it will give you a head start and increase the chances of your designer creating something that both you and your users will love.*

We'll start with a step-by-step overview of how to strategically map out the design of your app, then we'll follow it up with some of the best practices and no-gos for making your design shine.

Structuring Your App's Visual Design

It's time to roll up your sleeves and dive into the hands-on work of making your app a reality. This part of the framework requires more effort, but it will provide you with a comprehensive pathway to creating a visual representation of your app. Over the next few pages, I will guide you through a structured process to prioritize the visual components of your project, which will in turn create a foundational road map for its design.

Step 1: Create a User Flow

WHAT'S A USER FLOW?

User flows are visual representations of how a user will move through your app. Think of them as a map consisting of a series of elements—specifically arrows, diamonds, and rectangles—that outline your user's journey. User flows help you determine how many pages you'll need to complete all your specific tasks or functions in the app.

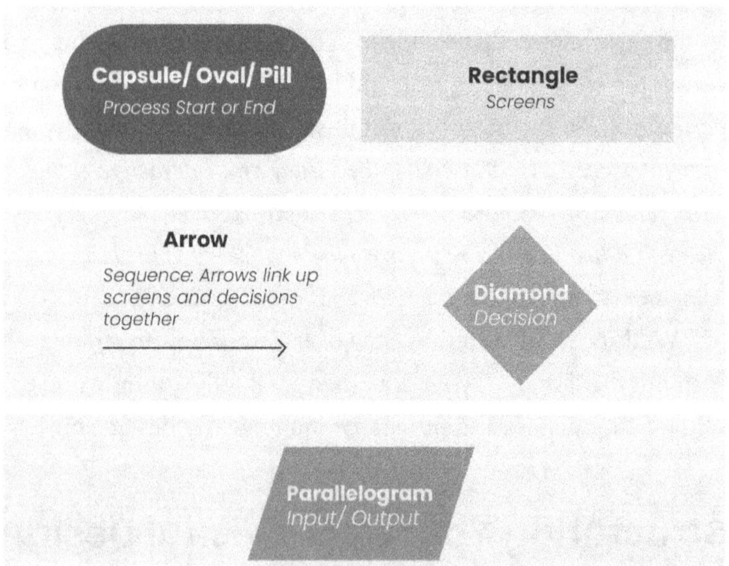

USER FLOW ELEMENTS

User flow elements are simply shapes that signify various actions within the app.

Rectangles	Rectangles are used to represent screens.
Diamonds	Diamonds are used to represent decisions (for example, tapping the login button, swiping to the left, zooming in).
Arrows	Arrows link up screens and decisions together.

Your user flow may look something like this:

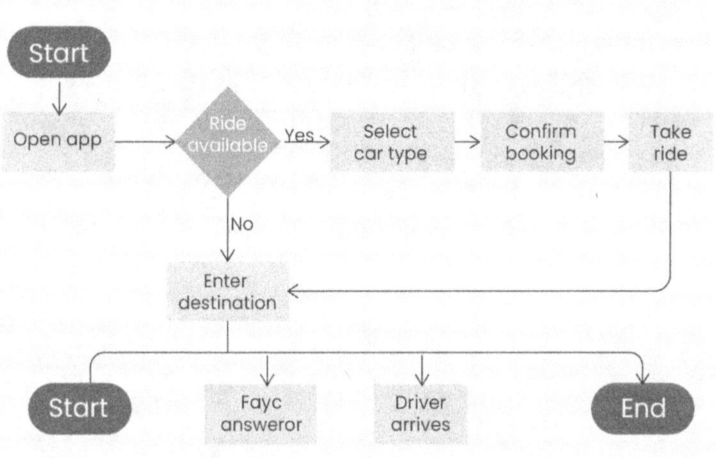

Use these references to begin organizing and sketching your app's user flow on paper or with the design tool of your choice. Though seemingly tedious work, this is a pivotal opportunity to streamline your users' experience in the app early.

Step 2: Sketch Your Wireframes

WHAT'S A WIREFRAME?

Wireframes are essentially app screen blueprints. They are 2D representations of the skeletal framework of each page of your app. You construct them to decide what elements to include on a page and where they each should go.

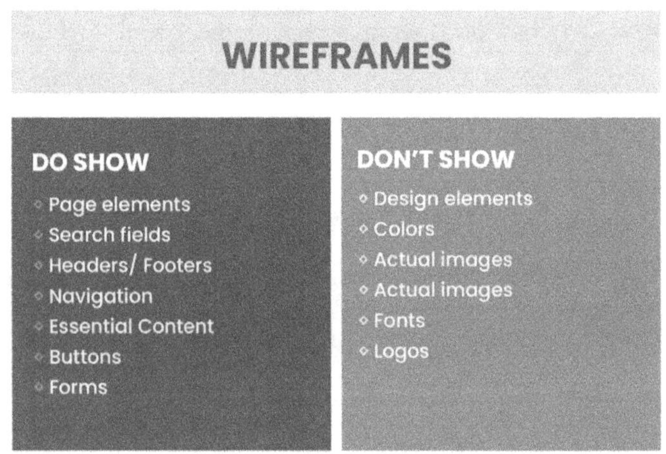

Wireframes provide a visual layout of elements to be included on a page or screen.

An Example of a Wireframe

Once you've mapped out your user flow, use it as a guide to begin sketching wireframes for each app screen—these screens correspond to the rectangles in your user flow diagram. In the template provided below, known as a *WireRequire, record each page's purpose, its key elements, and any necessary integrations to make it functional. This crucial step helps you create a detailed inventory of all the components needed to build your app, a process I refer to as wireframe cataloging. By the end of this step, you'll have a comprehensive list of all features and functionality required to turn your app concept into reality.* Your wire requirement notes will include the following:

1. *Objective:* The purpose of this screen (e.g., registration page)
2. *Essential elements and features:* Key features or functionality that should be included (e.g., buttons, forms, a sign-up/login option, forgot password link, brand logo at the top of the page)
3. *Integrations:* Any other software, solutions, or services required (e.g., option to sign in with Facebook or Gmail)

While these notes aren't necessarily part of the wireframe itself, they play a critical part in helping you prioritize what is essential versus nonessential on the front end of your app. They will be invaluable in detailing your product requirements to your designer and developers, ensuring your vision is accurately brought to life.

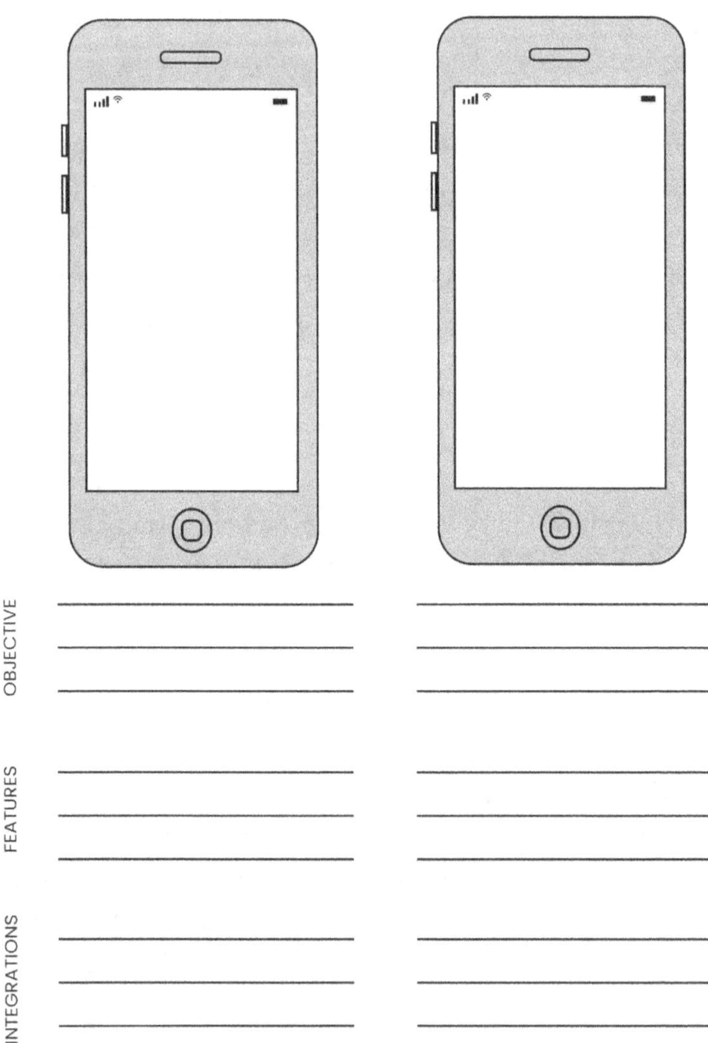

> *Wireframe cataloging, or the process of organizing and itemizing the features on each screen, will streamline your future design and development efforts.*

DEVELOPER INSIGHT

"Document your ideal process and write basic user personas to provide to the development team. Clients often have a lack of clarity on what the goal of each feature is and what value it adds to each user. I wish more clients had a process flow or diagram for the process that they are trying to achieve. Creating a pseudo-product road map would be helpful."

~Jermaine Henry, CEO of Norus Technologies[1]

APPRENEUR INSIGHT

"Take time to document everything. It may feel long and unnecessary at the beginning, but it will pay off in the long run. In addition, if you have an idea of what you want a certain screen or web page to look like, find something similar on the web and take screenshots. Use visual examples as much as possible. There are very few UI/UX ideas that don't already exist. Search the internet for sections of websites that you like particularly well and feed them to your developers. The less 'figuring out' a developer needs to do, the better. You would never have a contractor build you a house without very specific blueprints. Treat product development the same way."[2]

~Eric Sonnier, Executive Director, UVI RTPark

If you're more tech savvy, you may be wondering if you can create the wireframes digitally. The answer is yes, there are a number of great tools that can help you create amazing frames, but this activity at its core is a brainstorm—a doc dump to get all your ideas out of your head and put them in front of you on paper. I strongly encourage you to try the paper option first, then opt for the digital route.

If you find yourself struggling with how to make the designs look cool or sleek, stop, take a break, and open some of your favorite apps to find design inspiration. Take mental notes on how they followed the key considerations mentioned earlier and how you may be able to modify them to your own needs.

Take the pressure off! Remember, it's not your job to supply top-tier frames but rather to, only to provide the relevant information for your designer to run with.

Step 2: Conduct a Usability Test

Once you're done with your sketches, it's time to test them out!

There are dozens of online tools that allow you to automate this process, but I still prefer pen and paper. Call me old-fashioned.

If you go the physical route, you'll need to make paper copies of your wireframe with the notes sections removed. Cut them into individual pages and spread them out on the floor or a table to mimic your user flow diagram. Then invite a friend, family member, or colleague to come over and review what you've created to conduct a *usability test*.

A usability test is a method used to evaluate how easily and effectively users can interact with your app. The goal of this activity is to get another set of trusted eyes on your frames to gauge if the flow is intuitive to a first-time user and to note any issues or difficulties they encounter. As your tester explores your frames, allow them to ask questions and take note of their reactions, points of confusion, and commentary. This is an opportunity to garner feedback and make edits before you get too deep into the process.

Again, this can all be done online, but with so much time spent behind a screen, a little human interaction and person-to-person feedback couldn't hurt.

"Okay, so what happens next?"

After you've made any user feedback edits to your frames, you'll pick your color schemes and prepare relevant collateral such as photos, content, and videos that will exist in the app.

At this point you have the option of finding an independent app designer now or waiting until you hire your development team, who will likely offer design services alongside development.

If you opt for finding a designer first, you can turn these materials over to them to create a *mockup*—realistic renderings of what your app will eventually look like. Mockups are still flat images, but they can include logos, colors, and icons.

You will work with the designer to approve the final mockups so they can convert them into *a prototype*—a usable, interactive simulation of how a user will engage with the new product or feature.

An app starts with a wireframe, turns into a mockup, and then becomes a prototype.

After the prototype is drafted, I recommend organizing an informal but trusted focus group to conduct another usability test and collect feedback on the design. This can be a small group of family and friends or, if possible, your target audience. Allow them to run through the design without interference and, again, note any questions, confusion, or commentary they have when navigating it. Take notes, so you can repeat and refine the prototype with your designer before you finally hand the designs over to a developer.

With your solid design foundation in place, you can now focus on refining your app using these best practices:

Design Best Practices

Simplify Your Onboarding Experience

One in four mobile apps are abandoned after they are first opened. Another 77 percent of users abandon an app just seventy-two hours after download.[3]

You're probably guilty of it yourself. Think about it: How many times have you downloaded an app, opened it up, gotten overwhelmed by the first page or two, and just given up? Getting registered for an app shouldn't feel like rocket science.

One of the ways you can provide users with a friendly onboarding experience is by welcoming them with an *empty state*, or pages that require user input to proceed to next steps. Requiring users to populate small bits of data on empty pages can teach new users step-by-step how to use an app and what is to come—without the instant frustration.

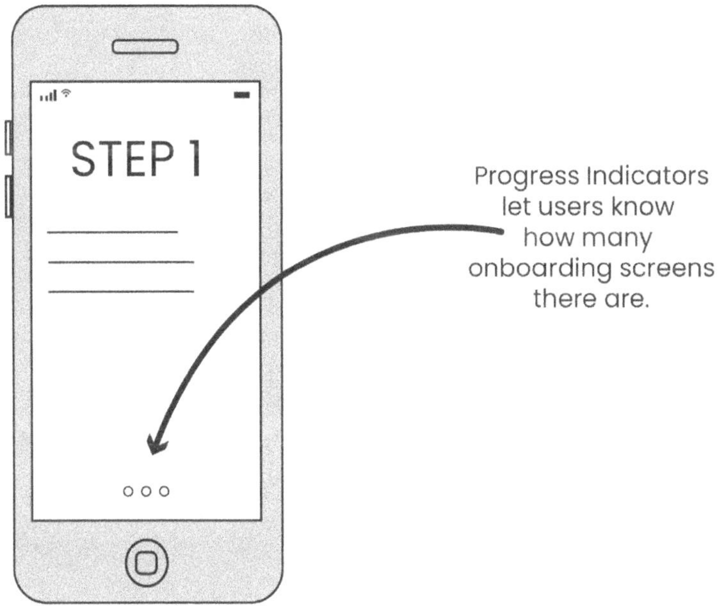

Help users understand how to use and onboard to your app with a simple, actionable process.

Gradually Introduce Features

Technical overwhelm is a real thing, and that's why it's critical to introduce the right product features at the right time. If you are asking users for information to onboard your app, you should only ask for that information when you need that information. If you must provide instructions for a feature, do it only when it's time to take that step. This process is called contextual onboarding.

As you begin to imagine what your app may feel like from page to page, continue to apply contextual onboarding. For example, if they don't need to upload a picture to begin using the app, why ask for access to a user's camera before it's necessary?

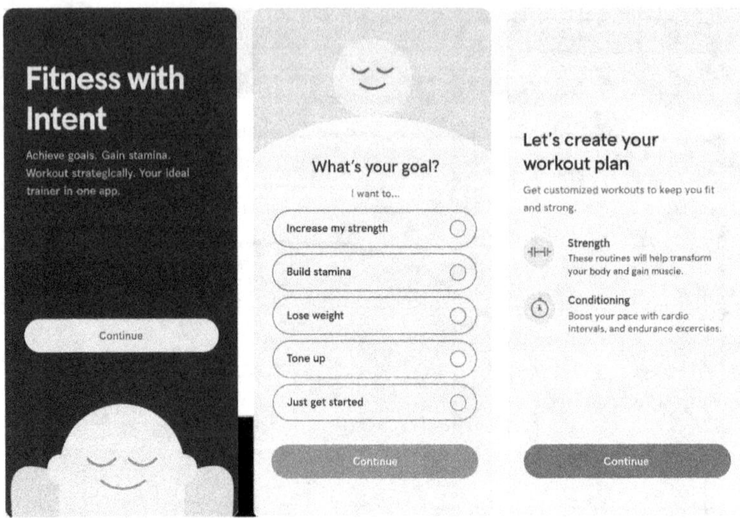

Users respond better to apps that provide information as they need it or as it's required to move forward.

Make Actions Bite-Sized

Even when you use contextual onboarding, there are times when you can't avoid long, tedious tasks in an app. You can, however, make them as digestible as possible by breaking them into bite-sized pieces. Think through how you can segment steps or the collection of information into smaller sections. Even if it's ultimately still lengthy, it will feel manageable to users and a necessary part of the process.

Cut Through the Clutter

When you're excited about your app, there's a natural inclination to try to squeeze in every feature possible . . . but this push to make it all fit can make your app feel clunky, cluttered, and hard to navigate.

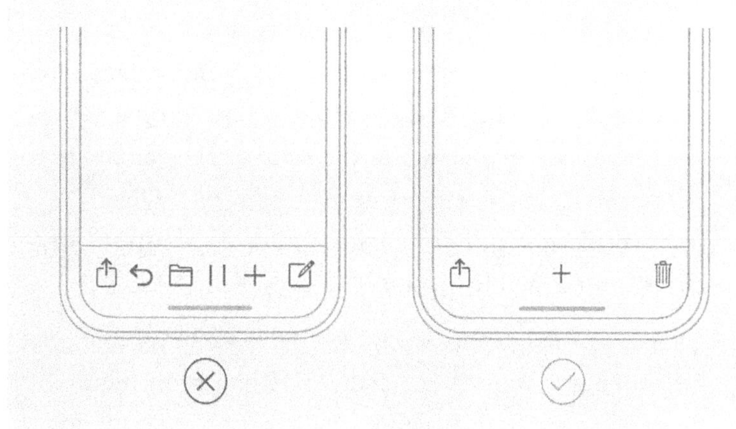

Avoid flooding your app screens with too many features or functions.

If your core functionality is robust, I encourage you to lean on your designer. A seasoned user experience designer will be able to look at your product with fresh eyes and integrate core elements in lean, innovative ways that are dimension-friendly and easy on the eyes.

Design for Fingers

This seems like a no-brainer, but it's a very common mistake: Design your mobile app with room for fingers, not for a cursor.

When you start mapping out your app, you'll likely design its pages on a computer screen, but you must remember that users will likely be visiting your app via mobile phone. This means they won't have a tiny little mouse cursor to make selections or take actions, so you'll need to design for the width of their fingers and provide the space they'll need to select elements with ease.

Early in my career I worked at an e-commerce start-up where I ran the customer support department. One day a customer called in and requested a refund on a series of purchases. The reason for the return? He claimed the purchase was accidental because he had "FAT FINGERS" (his words, not mine) and had pressed "confirm purchase" on the app by mistake.

Now while I'm sure his fingers were rather plump . . . his purchases weren't accidental. He had been required to sign off on four separate confirmation pages before completing his purchases.

But let this story be a light and friendly reminder to keep all the fluffy fingers in mind as you navigate your designs.

DESIGN FOR FINGERS

Not a cursor

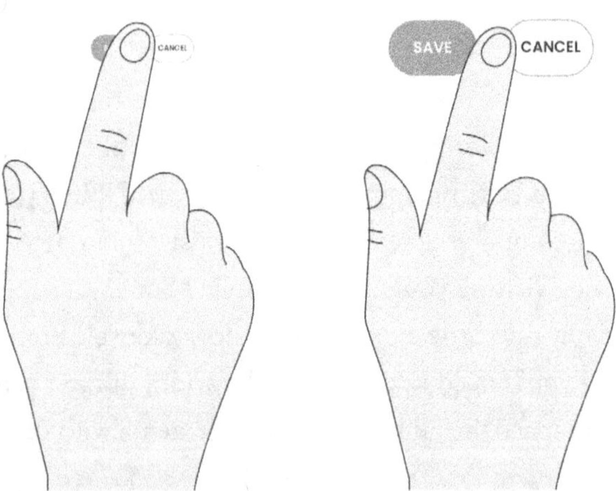

Remember, users will be scrolling with their fingers, not a cursor. Design accordingly.

Navigations Should Always Be Visible

Think about the apps you use most frequently, like Facebook, Instagram, or even your email. Is there ever a point where you can't see your navigation or can't figure out how to get back to where you started from? Very rarely. Your users should never find it difficult to find their way back home.

Leverage Device Capabilities

Smartphones are actually very powerful tools. When utilized correctly, they can be a helpful partner in optimizing experiences in your app. As this relates to design, there will be many features or pages you won't have to incorporate into the product because your phone already has these capacities; you simply need to contextually ask your user for access. For instance, iOS devices offer biometric authentication like FaceID or TouchID, and Android devices provide similar features through fingerprint scanning or facial recognition. Both platforms also support push notifications, GPS for location services, and cameras that can be used for augmented reality or scanning QR codes. Start brainstorming on which features and elements in your app are already provided by an iOS or Android device. Consider how you can take advantage of them while saving space and cutting costs.

Now that we've identified some best practices, let's quickly run through the things to avoid:

Poor Design Habits

- *ALL CAPS:* It's just annoying. It makes people feel like you're screaming at them through the phone.

- *Long-form text:* Attention spans are short. Long-form content can be a deterrent and a visual strain for mobile users.
- *Gated walls:* Unless gated walls are part of your business model, think twice about creating artificial barriers that gate or isolate people from access. In select cases, they can build anticipation for users, but they mostly tend to spark frustration and anxiety.

When we first launched CultureCrush, we decided to have a series of waitlist walls where we would gate access to the app based on location. In the dating app world, 5,000 is sort of a magic number; it's said to be the number of users you'll need in one city for the app to really begin to thrive. If the volume of users is under this number regionally, users will generally run out of match options quickly and instantly lose interest in the app.

Our strategy was to gate every city, excluding the ones where we knew we would be guaranteed to meet our magic number. As other cities hit their magic number, we would instantly unlock them, granting access to all on the waitlist. We thought this would help us consolidate our marketing efforts and centralize our attention to where there was demand for the product.

It made sense in theory, but it was a totally different story in practice.

As luck would have it, we immediately saw growth in some unanticipated markets. These cities showed incredible promise but were just shy of the magic number. And while we were thrilled about the traction, our users in these cities were furious that they had used their data to download this app they could not access .... but were also afraid to delete the app because they feared losing their place on the waitlist. We had left them in dating app purgatory.

They flooded our app store reviews with negative comments about how the app didn't work, despite us providing them with clear information in the app about the gate being lifted as soon as their city reached 5,000 users.

It was a huge setback for us, which ultimately resulted in us lifting all the gates. You live and you learn, but the gates were a feature we probably could have done without or at least done differently!

As we wrap up this chapter, use the checklist below to get ahead on each element of the design process, keeping the best practices top of mind. By completing these steps, you'll set yourself up for success as you move into the development phase.

Chapter checklist

- ☐ Create a user flow diagram.
- ☐ With your user flow as a reference, create wireframes.
- ☐ Create a wireframe catalog.
- ☐ Conduct a usability test with one or more trusted testers and log their feedback.
- ☐ Create a mockup (optional).
- ☐ Create a prototype (optional).
- ☐ Conduct a focus group (optional).

CHAPTER 8

Development Prep

Developers regularly tell me that the biggest deterrent to completing a project is not money or lack of skill; it's client clarity. This chapter aims to ensure both you and your team will have a clear and comprehensive outlook on what you're striving to accomplish, starting with the app's requirements.

Requirements are single statements of something the app or product should do. They detail the *features and functionality the app needs to operate effectively and be a problem-solving tool.*[1]

Requirements are necessary in many different scenarios, even outside of app development. Take, for example, building a new shed in your backyard. Before you begin building a shed, you'd consider such elements as the following:

- *Dimensions:* What size shed can reasonably fit in the space?
- *Utility:* Will it require electricity or plumbing?
- *Aesthetic:* Does it match the home's existing exterior paint scheme?
- *Materials:* Should you use weather-resistant materials?

- *Budget:* What type of unit can you afford at this time?
- *Timeline:* How quickly do you need to complete this project? Is winter or the rainy season around the corner?

These parameters influence not only what you can build, but how you can build it. And while you may have an array of options, ultimately you must build within this scope. App development is no different. Your requirements are the benchmarks for outlining the design and development of the solution.

Requirements are detailed across a product requirements document and are often broken down into the following common categories and subcategories:

- *Business requirements:* Statements surrounding the app's business model, monetization, and how admins may need to manage it
- *User or stakeholder requirements:* Remember our personas? This is where their requests and needs for an app come in handy.
- *Functional:* Relates directly to how the features of the product should work
- *Nonfunctional:* These requirements tend to be unrelated to the problem the app seeks to solve. They typically center on the maintenance and sustainability of the product and may include things like scalability or security.
- *User interface:* All aesthetic-related requirements like branding, color choices, or logo usage fall under this category.
- *System requirements:* These are the stipulations surrounding the software that your app needs to operate.

Other requirements categories may include security to safeguard the app, performance testing to evaluate load time, and device-specific testing to ensure the app works the same across different phone versions and device types.

Here are a few examples of what various requirements might look like for a food delivery app:

- *Functionality testing:* Ensure users can browse through the app's menu, select items, and add them to the cart.
- *Usability testing:* Evaluate the app's user interface for intuitiveness and ease of navigation when placing an order.
- *Performance testing:* Evaluate how the app performs on various devices and operating systems.
- *Security and privacy testing:* Assess the app's handling of user data, ensuring that personal and payment information is secure.

REQUIREMENTS EXAMPLES

Business requirement	Enable freelancers and small business owners to file taxes more efficiently.
Market requirement	Integrate with the IRS tax filing system
Functional requirement	Provide real-time income and expense tracking
Non-functional requirement	Ensure the application performs reliably under heavy load.

If the requirements were WHAT a product should do, a specification document details HOW it should be done. A *specification* document (or spec sheet) details individual requirements and how to achieve them. Spec sheets typically describe the application from the perspective of the technical team. Although there is a distinct difference between the two, many people use *product requirements docs* and *spec sheets* interchangeably as they tend to complement one another.

Now, this is the part where doing your homework pays off. If you took the time to complete chapter 7's wireframe cataloging activity, you already have a major head start on listing the requirements, features, and functionality you want to include in your app.

The natural next step here is to consolidate each of the elements, key features, and integrations you listed below each of your wireframes into one comprehensive requirements document.

But before we do, I'd like to remind you that we're still striving to create an MVP of your app—the leanest, most simple version of your product to test with your audience. The more requirements and features you have, the more costly this will be to build. Prioritizing features can be a tough task because each requirement may *feel* like it plays a key part in your vision. However, feelings aren't necessarily facts. Ask yourself: Do you really want to spend thousands more on an array of features that aren't essential to proving your concept or running your business and that you aren't 100 percent sure your customers will love? It's a big risk to take!

APPRENEUR INSIGHT

"When it comes to building a start-up, perfect product specifications don't exist; things change too rapidly. Help the dev team understand the why and where you are hoping to get to. Then guide them to fill in on the how."[2]

~Dan Kihanya, Director REI Path Ahead Ventures, Creator of Founders Unfound Podcast

To make the selection process a little easier I'd like to introduce you to the *MoSCoW method*,[3] a prioritization technique that helps you trim the fat by categorizing every one of your app's requirements into four categories.

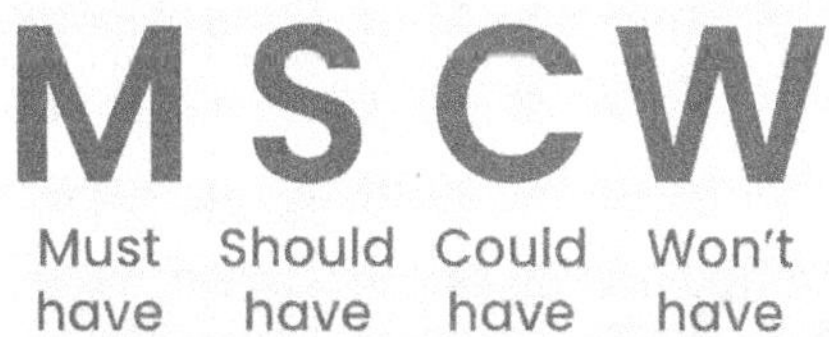

Your *must-haves* are your nonnegotiables; you need them to run the app, to be compliant, and for the app to be legal or make money.

Then you have your *should-haves*; these are requirements that would be amazing features, but they're simply not vital. The difference between them and the next category is that they tend to be points of distinction and differentiators, but at the end of the day, they're still not essential to the bottom line of your app.

Could-haves are nice complements, but they're just garnishes to your musts and should-haves. If you find you have extra money in the budget, these could be good add-ons.

And lastly, the *won't haves—at this time*; these are features and components that are completely out of budget and that you likely just have an affinity for. The "won't-haves" column can feel like the kiss of death for a feature, but putting them in this column doesn't mean they're gone for good; they can always be revisited later.

DEVELOPER INSIGHT

"One of the biggest client challenges is a lack of priorities. Most clients think about features but never prioritize them by importance or value."[4]

~Jermaine Henry, CEO of Norus Technologies

Reference your wireframe catalog and begin to prioritize all the features and functionalities you wrote in your notes section in the following chart.

M	S	C	W

As you start to prioritize, please look over this short list of commonly overlooked elements and features that first-time app builders often forget but may be very helpful to the management and maintenance of your app:

- *Content management system (CMS):* You may remember discussing this as a key term in chapter 5. If your app includes a content feature, consider having your developers create a web-based content management system (CMS) alongside your app. This allows you to easily update and edit content without needing to change the app's code each time—an essential convenience. Without this CMS dashboard, updating your app would mean tampering with the code every single time, and honestly, who has time for that?
- *Admin panel:* Similar to the CMS, the admin panel provides you with site-wide control of your app. This is where you can manage features, review users, track data, and toggle settings on and off without having to edit the base code of the app.
- *Security measures:* If you're collecting user data, consider what steps or tools you have taken to protect this information.

If you complete the MoSCoW activity and have more than 70 percent of your notes in the must-have column, then you are likely not being lean enough and run the risk of adding too much to your MVP. It may take a few rounds but strive to make the tough decisions surrounding what is truly a priority and what is not.

APPRENEUR INSIGHT

"... Make sure that you include the entire vision of your app in every phase of your implementation thinking. You typically can't achieve everything at once and so some things will need to be put off to later. Prioritize features in a way that you ensure that you are keeping the later phases in mind. Lots of people make the mistake of putting in the highest-value item now and forgetting about the plan they made for later, then later comes around and it becomes prohibitively more difficult to implement items you had planned at the initial conception of your idea. Keep your road map in your thoughts at every phase of your project."[5]

~Barney Spann, VP of Technology, Partner at Carperks (acquired by TrueCar, Inc.)

The Requirements Document of Your Product

After you've identified and streamlined your must-haves, put your functional and nonfunctional requirements into a product requirements document. Now I know this seems tedious and you're probably thinking, Amanda, I just outlined them—why am I itemizing them again?

When you meet with prospective developers, one of the first things they're going to ask you to provide is a requirements document sheet. You will need to either provide it to them or complete a form or template so they can compose it for you. They need this document to accurately determine if they can build what you're asking for, outline a solution for you, and provide you with an estimate of how much it will cost to build. While many people choose to do this alongside the development team, I think it's helpful to prepare your own draft ahead of meeting with them to expedite the process. That said, recognize that your developers are experts and stay open to their recommendations or suggestions that may help you achieve your goal in new ways.

Use the following template to outline and identify the following:

- *The type of application you want:* mobile, web, smart TV, desktop?
- *The device or platform you want it to display on:* If it's a mobile app, for example, iOS or Android? If it's an extension, which browsers?
- *User roles:* Perhaps you have different user types that will be utilizing the app. If you're launching a marketplace, for example, you'll need user roles for buyers, sellers, and for yourself as the admin.
- *Business requirements:* Clearly define your app's business model, including the vision for the company and revenue streams such as in-app purchases or ads. The more developers understand about how the business operates, the better they can make strategic recommendations for its structure, ensuring alignment on both the business and product front.
- *Functional requirements:* List the key features and actions the app must have to work as intended.
- *Nonfunctional requirements:* Identify other key considerations for the app to be successful.

To prepare for your developers, detail your requirements here or on a separate document.

Requirement	
Business Requirement	
Market Requirement	
Functional Requirement	
Non-Functional Requirement	

A product Requirements Sheet

Woop-woop! With the completion of your product requirements document, you're now free to enter the third phase of the framework, where we will begin your developer search. Are you excited to start building your team?

- ☐ Revisit or outline your wireframe requirements.
- ☐ Conduct a MoSCoW prioritization.
- ☐ Complete draft product requirements document.

CHAPTER 9

Building Your Dev Team

If you have decided to use an agency for your app, you can anticipate working with a small team that's likely to include the following people:

- A project or product manager
- A user interface/user experience designer
- One or more iOS developers
- One or more Android developers
- A quality assurance manager

The *project manager* will be your primary contact and liaison between you and the development team. Their top objective is to oversee the project, ensuring that the team meets its milestones and navigates any miscommunications or roadblocks along the way with ease.

User interface (UI) and user experience (UX) designers spearhead the visual elements of the app. The UI designer helps to conceptualize the screens and pages users will interact with, while the UX designer works to ensure that the flow of the app itself is intuitive and user-friendly. If you had your app designed before finding your agency, you may not interact with these team members as much.

Since most developers have a specialty, your agency will probably assign an engineer to work on each platform in tangent. You may see both a front-end and back-end developer actively working on their respective parts of the app to bring your vision to life. Occasionally, you get to work with *a full stack developer*, or someone who can work cross-functionality on both the front and back end or "the full stack" of technology. These folks are pretty much the Swiss army knives of development.

If your project is on the larger side, you may have an extended team that includes up to three or more people in each of these roles as well as a *quality assurance engineer or tester*. This person will monitor each part of the app to ensure it doesn't contain any bugs, adapts to all its respective device types, and that the end product meets all the requirements you set for the team.

In this lesson, we'll be highlighting things that should be top of mind as you begin your hiring process. I'll outline places you can find technical talent, the best practices for engaging them, and interview tips to find the right agency for you.

How Do I Find an Agency?

To find an agency, let's start online.

Freelance Communities and Marketplaces

Online freelance and marketplace communities are dedicated to matchmaking you with diverse development talent. They give you the ability to provide a short description of your project and then set search parameters—including your budget, category of work, location, and more—to narrow your search. Freelancers and agencies alike search for new work on these platforms and can be contacted through them if they are a good fit for your project.

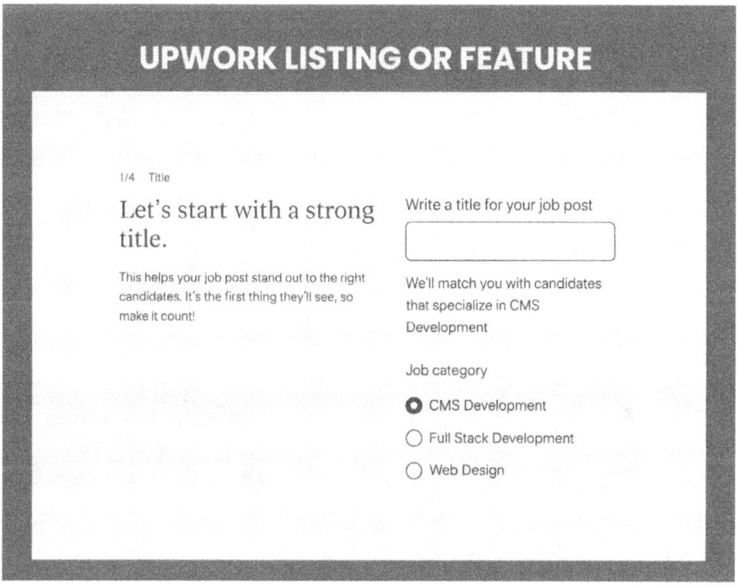

UPWORK LISTING OR FEATURE

1/4 Title

Let's start with a strong title.

This helps your job post stand out to the right candidates. It's the first thing they'll see, so make it count!

Write a title for your job post

We'll match you with candidates that specialize in CMS Development

Job category

CMS Development

Full Stack Development

Web Design

Using a platform like Upwork could instantly connect you with dozens of prospective agencies but with so many candidates available, quality can be hard to measure. When you find an agency you like, you'll need to do your part to vet and interview them to ensure they're the right fit. I will show you how shortly.

Design Communities and Creative Networks

In recent years, new online creative design communities and networks have emerged. The platforms aim to help people showcase and discover creative work. You can find not only amazing design inspiration here but also great technical talent who are looking for their next big project.

Your Social Media Page

"But, Amanda, I don't know anyone who develops apps . . ."
You may not, but someone in your network probably does. Update your status by asking for recommendations for an app developer; you may be surprised at who responds!

Plus, developers and agencies are getting a lot savvier with their lead generation and have begun to search platforms like X and Instagram for people who are looking for their services.

Here's an example of a tweet I posted about how I wanted to rebuild my personal website, and a proactive company from the other side of the world responded to the call.

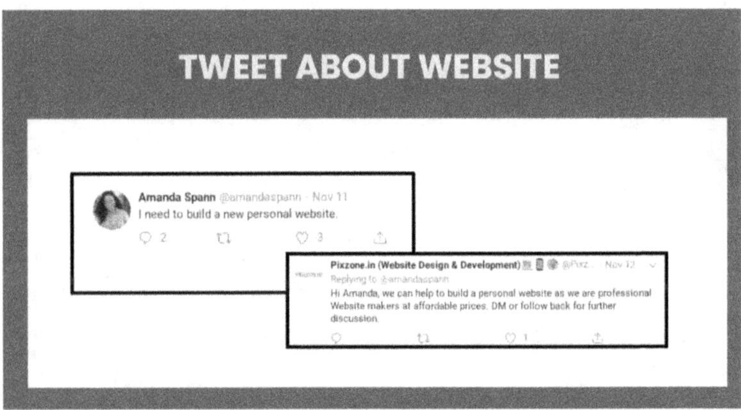

Outside of posts, there are also massive Facebook groups of developers and designers who are always looking for new projects. If you join these groups, the admins will guide you on when and what you can post and how you may solicit new talent.

Now, let's move to in-person.

Meet-Up Groups

If you're apprehensive about working with someone you met online, you may be better off building a rapport with someone face-to-face at an in-person meet-up group. Search for developer meet-ups in your city and start networking at their events. If you're nontechnical, I know going to these events may feel intimidating, but I assure you most people there will admire your courage and welcome you with open arms.

Start-Up Events

Start-up events can range from hackathons, where developers are coding new products overnight, to panels to workshops that focus on building your entrepreneurial skill sets. Search event platforms or boards for upcoming start-up and entrepreneurial events in a city near you.

Co-working Spaces

With remote work here to stay, most cities have at least one entrepreneurship or co-working center where workers from different companies collectively share office space and business resources. These collaboration hubs often have an assortment of freelance and agency talent working in or around them, as well as job boards you can post and recruit on. Additionally, it couldn't hurt to join a space to get access to business development classes to grow and scale your app.

Colleges and Universities

Local colleges and universities are a great place to find up-and-coming talent. Students and student groups are often willing to work for a fraction of the price of a seasoned development team, and they may even be able to earn college credit for lending their support. If you reach out to computer science professors or a college's career center, they will walk you through how to conduct student outreach.

Any or all of these communities are sure to help you find some promising leads. But once you find the right fit, you should start preparing yourself to pay them for their time.

How Much Is Development Going to Cost Me?

Early in the book, we briefly discussed how agencies typically charge hourly for their services. When estimating the cost of your app, each feature will be reviewed and assigned an estimated number of development hours. These hours will then be grouped into project milestones. To get your estimated total cost, multiply the hourly rate by the total number of hours.

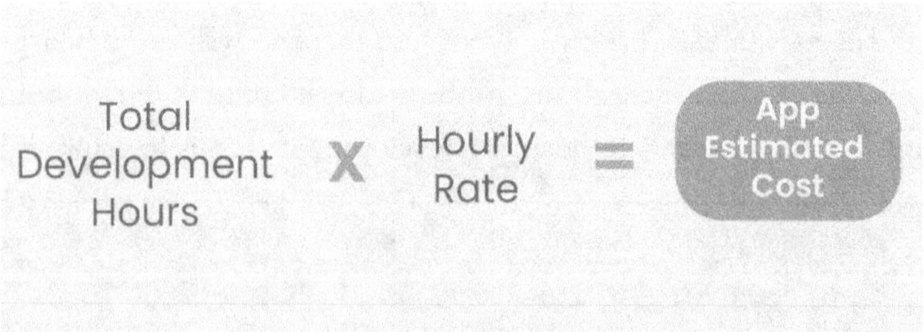

Total Development Hours X Hourly Rate = App Estimated Cost

If you're not in a position to pay the total cost of your project upfront, don't worry. As mentioned earlier in the book, development projects are typically paid in installments or through payment plans. This structure protects both you and the developers. For example, if you can no longer pay the remaining balance, the developers can halt the project. Conversely, if you're not satisfied with the developers' work midway through, you won't have to continue paying for unfinished or unsatisfactory work.

While there are typically no fees associated with the interview process or for providing an estimate, developers charge their various rates during the development process for good reasons. Factors that affect these fees are as follows:

- *Experience and expertise:* You wouldn't typically expect to pay someone with six months' experience the same salary as someone who's been in the industry for eight years, would you? Developers raise their rates with experience and as they become domain experts in particular fields.
- *Complexity:* If the features and functionality of your project require the agency to dedicate more resources to it, they will likely have to raise the rate to pay additional staff members.
- *Location:* Outsourcing overseas, or the practice of contracting a team in another country, has become popular because you can often acquire quality work for a fraction of domestic prices. Due to exchange rates and cost of living, many overseas developers typically don't feel a need to charge as much as Western developers do. Take a look at the ranges of typical rates you may see across continents:

AVERAGE OUTSORCING RATES BY REGION

Eastern Europe - $ 27-42 per hour.

Asia- $ 20-45 per hour

Latin America- $ 35-55 per hour.

Africa- $ 20-45 per hour.

Note that these rates are an estimated average but not the rule. There are developers in India, South Africa, Argentina, and many other parts of the world who charge just as much as American developers because they have the skills and experience to command the rate. I've had amazing experiences with developers around the world. Price or location doesn't always determine quality of work, but everyone's experience is different.

APPRENEUR INSIGHT

"I spent money on overseas contractors and received very little output. I assumed they were quality because they were vetted by a platform that sourced engineers throughout South America. Maybe they were good, but they weren't spending as much time on my project as they said they were.

I should've trusted my gut and fired them immediately, but it was hard to find quality, reasonably priced engineers at the time. I knew if I let them go, it would be weeks of searching to find other engineers, and my internal team of engineers were past the point of burnout. I was hoping they'd clean up their act after I told them they weren't producing enough. The situation didn't get much better after those conversations. I ended up letting them go shortly after. If I could go back, I wouldn't let the fear of not finding engineers fast enough cloud my judgment on which engineers to hire. And if I avoid that, I'm hopefully not in the position to make my second mistake of not firing them fast enough."[1]

~Eric Sonnier, Executive Director, UVI RTPark

How Do I Create a Developer Job Listing?

Now that we know where to find developers and what we should be prepared for, let's start seeking out and interviewing them.

If you're posting a project listing on a job board or marketplace, include these elements:

- *A clear and concise title:* Similar to the subject line of an email, give a high-level overview of the project and what type of professional services you're looking for.
- *A short description of the project:* You don't have to give away your big idea here, but you do need to give the development teams some color and context into what you're building and how you want it built. Include details like the following:
- Category of app
- Monetization methods

- Platforms
- Critical features or functionality

Be sure to request samples of their work, in particular apps that are currently active or in the same or similar category of your project.

- *Your budget:* For the purposes of negotiation, I don't recommend you post your budget if you can help it. You should know it, but you don't necessarily have to post it. If the listing requires you post a number, set a reasonable lower rate—big enough to get their attention but small enough so that you don't get overcharged. Mention in your project description that the rate is simply a placeholder, and teams are welcome to counter with their estimated rate. Remember, more expensive doesn't mean better, but you also get what you pay for. Be willing to invest in your dream, but be mindful and strategic about not breaking the bank.
- *Time commitment:* Set a reasonable timeline for when you'd like to start and ideally finish your app. As you may recall from earlier in the book, depending on the size and scale of a project, app timelines can range from a few weeks to several months. Be mindful to set a sensible and realistic timeline.

INVESTOR INSIGHT

On the biggest mistake founders make in the product development process . . .

"They either underestimate how much time it will take (more common) or overcomplicate it and take forever to launch. There are stages and MVPs for a reason, so truly being realistic and understanding and defining what should be at each stage is key."[2]

~Nichole Yembra, Chief Problem Solver at The Chrysalis KO

A developer listing may look something along the lines of

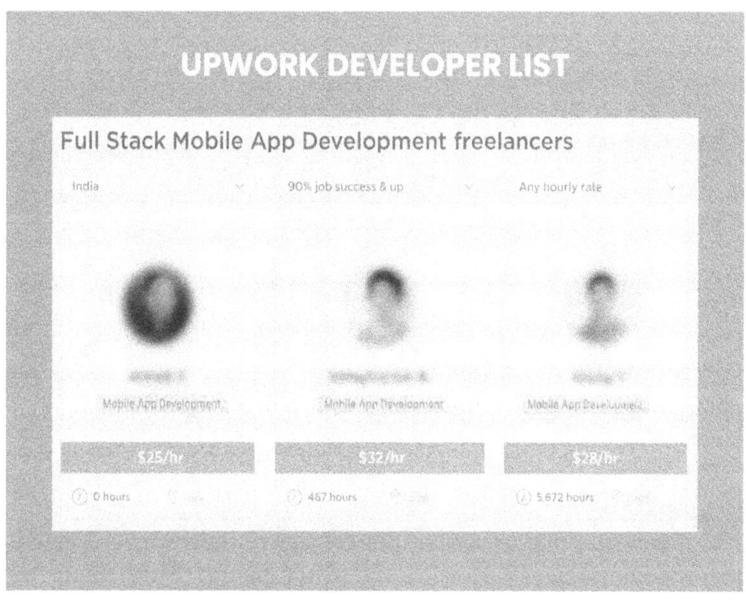

Here is another example of a more detailed listing I used for another app I co-founded, TipOff—Word Guessing Game. You'll notice I was pretty detailed with the product description because TipOff was already a live product when we sought to bring a new development lead onto the team. If this had been a new product I was still ideating on, I probably would have simply described the app idea as a "word guessing game."

TipOff CTO

Vision:

With a goal of disrupting the lack of diversity in mobile entertainment, TipOff App is a word guessing game for the culture. Similar to the board game Taboo, the app requires that players describe the word at the top of the card without saying the 5 remaining words at the bottom. The game can be customized with assorted word packs like Church or HBCUs.

We are striving to to position TipOff as a leading point of culture connectivity between the black and minority communities and the brands, organizations and corporations that hope to interact with them . We are seeking a CTO to help us build, grow and expand our product for long term sustainability and profitability.

Responsibilities:

- Leading product development and design of app
- Ongoing maintenance and mitigation of updates, errors, bugs, updates and extensions
- Spearheading the framing, building and testing of new in-app capabilities, services or features as required

The Ideal Candidate:

- Has the ability to manage a team in office and remote
- Ability to communicate and interface with technical and non-technical members of the organization. Should be self-motivated and can lead projects independently while keeping non-technical teammates up-to-speed in an effective manner
- Full stack development capabilities with familiarity and emphasis on technologies such as HTML5,PHP, Objective C, Javascript, React, Redux and Node.js or Java services
- Is competent in Cross Platform Native App Development like React Native for iOS and Android platforms
- Will have the ability to understand technology deeply, dive in, and debug at any level in a software stack
- Is adaptable. Candidate should have previously been a startup founder, worked in a startup, or hacked on cutting edge projects while navigating uncharted territory.

Once you submit your listing, you may start to receive inquiries from interested parties who will want to learn more about you and your project. Upon reviewing their responses, first assess whether they followed the instructions listed in your posting and, if so, begin to review their work, as well as any testimonials they may have on their website or profile.

If you can, narrow the responses down to three to five teams and schedule a video call with each of them. This is your opportunity to get a feel for them and their communication style, and for them to get clarity around your app and to show you additional examples of their work.

Ahead of the video call, prepare a list of questions that are relevant to your project. Here are some sample questions:

- Can you provide a list of past and current customers?
- Will I get round-the-clock support?

- How many team members will be dedicated to my project?
- Based on the project I described, how would you go about building it?
- Do you offer payment plans?
- How do you handle post-development maintenance?
- Are you willing to sign a nondisclosure agreement as well as a development agreement?

How Will I Know They're the Right Team for Me?

Finding the right development team is more of an art than a science, but here are some key considerations to guide you in the direction of the right fit for you.

- *Technical skill:* There is no one-size-fits-all approach to building an app. Search for teams that are proactive, forward-thinking, and with a proven track record of relevant product development. Ask for their portfolio and published products so you can see live examples of their work.
- *Niche or specialties:* Strive to find development agencies that focus on your app category. I've met developers who only build insurance marketplaces or solely focus on emoji apps. If you've dreamed of it, there's probably someone who specializes in it.
- *Communication:* One of the biggest challenges of hiring overseas talent is language barriers. When it comes to explaining technology, patience is the name of the game as a lot of things can get lost in translation. You want an agency that you can effortlessly communicate with, but that also

has a healthy pace of correspondence. Beware of those who rush decisions or contact you excessively, demanding urgent replies or pressuring you to commit without thorough due diligence, as well as those who may ghost you or go unreasonable amounts of time without checking in.

- *Flexibility of fees:* You should anticipate paying for your app in installments as portions of it get completed. There should be complete transparency surrounding how many hours a feature might take to build, when it is expected to be delivered, and how much you have agreed to pay upon completion. If an agency quotes you a flat rate without itemizing fees or services, buyer beware.
- *After-development support:* Seek agencies that not only give a great development experience but also offer a plan to maintain your app after release. Many companies will offer up to six months' worth of ongoing support and post-deployment retainer plans.

After the interviews, you will likely know what team you feel most comfortable with. Honor what you see, but also trust your gut. Who do you honestly feel you will have the best chance of success with?

APPRENEUR INSIGHT

"I've had previous experience in sales roles and hiring employees, so I treated the process of finding a development team the same. I researched prospects, created a matrix to help me rank the candidates after interviews. I asked advisors and mentors to review the final candidates for second or third opinions, then I selected who I felt was the best fit. Red flags to look out for are teams that are slow to respond to your emails, teams that want to sell you their services rather than listening to what you need and creating a plan that fits your needs, teams that charge too much, teams that immediately want equity in your company, and teams that have language barriers with no representative who can effectively communicate or translate with you and for you."[3]

~Chris Davis, CEO at Fansub

APPRENEUR INSIGHT

"You really never know whether you have selected the right person or team. It's hard to tell from a resume. Screening is key to not wasting your time. When performing the actual interview you want to ensure that not only are they talented, but that they work well within a team setting. The best way to find this out is reviewing the work they have done.in the past and especially when working with others. If you're working with an agency, ask to have the exact team members who will be working on your project to participate in the interview. Be sure to prep beforehand and don't be afraid to ask challenging follow-up questions when something is not clear. You want to ensure you are getting to the root essence of the talent of the people being interviewed and how they respond to the pressure of a challenge."[4]

~Barney Spann, VP of Technology, Partner at Carperks (Acquired)

If this is your first time working with a developer, you may want to start with a test project as opposed to committing the entire app to them. This could be a small portion of your app project, like designing the prototype, just to see how you work together.

Depending on how the test project goes, either move forward with the next steps in the development process or rinse and repeat the search process. Sometimes it takes a few times to get it right, but it's better to take your time and find the right fit than feel the pain of the wrong choice later.

Chapter checklist

- ☐ Conduct online and/or in-person developer search.
- ☐ Create development job listing.
- ☐ Draft and outline interview questions.
- ☐ Arrange and schedule video conference interviews.

CHAPTER 10

Onboarding Your Development Agency

I remember finding my first development partner. Instead of breathing a sigh of relief, I was a bundle of nerves. On one hand, I was excited to be on the verge of bringing my idea to life; on the other, I was overwhelmed with anxiety. I had never developed anything before and was clueless about what was next or how I would manage the unknown.

Kicking Off Your App's Development

One thing is for sure: You'll be more prepared than I was when entering your development phase. This third step of iD3 consists of three distinct parts: analysis, design handoff, and implementation.

Analysis

The initial phase of app development involves thorough planning to lay a solid foundation for the project, ensuring a well-structured and strategically sound approach to building your product.

If you did your homework, you have already made significant progress by gathering requirements and collaborating with your developers to outline the technical specifications. If everything has gone according to plan, your chosen developers should now be providing you with a detailed scope or statement of work. This document should include suggestions for the tech stacks and solutions your app could be built on, a product delivery timeline, and a list of the project's expected deliverables.

Now, you may find that you're in complete alignment with the recommended plan, but in the event you have some questions or concerns, let me remind you: *You have the control here.*

This is your opportunity to speak to your dev team's business analyst or project manager and express your concerns about anything that doesn't sit well with you *before the coding starts.* Keep in mind that your project will inevitably evolve over time, but at this point it is not too late to take a step back and reconfigure.

Once you feel complete confidence in the plan, proceed with having your development team sign a nondisclosure agreement and development agreement.

As a refresher, **a nondisclosure agreement (NDA) establishes a confidential relationship between two parties in which they agree that the information shared, discussed, or obtained between them won't be made available to anyone else.**

You'll find that most dev shops will happily sign an NDA to ensure that they have your business. Occasionally you may get some pushback from firms who work on similar projects, as signing an NDA or a noncompete might overlap with related work they do. But don't worry, though these agreements are optional, practicing discretion and client confidentiality is generally seen as a best practice across the industry.

The development agreement, however, is nonnegotiable. If your development team is not willing to sign an agreement, you should end the relationship immediately. A *development agreement, also known as a software development or service agreement, is a legally enforceable contract that governs the provision of software development services. This service agreement outlines the relationship between you and your development partner, sets the terms of ownership, and details mutual expectations, obligations, and each party's responsibility. It protects both parties and provides guidance for next steps in the event there is a breach of contract.*

Development agreements should include the previously mentioned *statement of work (SOW)*. This is a project management document that clarifies and defines each project component, including, but not limited to, the product itself, its milestones, scheduling and timelines, payments, and acceptance criteria for deliverables.

When, and only when, these documents are countersigned and delivered will it be time to start the project. Once done, feel free to send the team your deposit and get the ball rolling.

DEVELOPER INSIGHT

On the biggest mistake founders make when they're developing or designing a product . . .

"The biggest point of development congestion is analysis paralysis. It can be tough to give your final say on something that you know is likely going to be changing over time through iterations. To prevent this, just try to get comfortable being uncomfortable. Nothing about entrepreneurship or product development is comfortable. Things are going to change. Things are going to break. It's your job as the client to keep the ball moving forward. So, if timeline is your most important variable, then you need to move forward even if you're not 100 percent comfortable with the design because you know that you'll be able to make future iterations. If cost is the most important, then it probably makes sense to take a bit more time during design to really clean things up to ensure that you reduce future needs of iteration."

~David Pawlan, Co-Founder at Aloa[1]

INVESTOR INSIGHT

"Scope creep. Founders are often pulled in different directions based on what's trendy or buzzy. For example, if you are developing an app right now, you may feel pressure to pivot to AI to meet the moment. There's power in the pivot but pivoting too often leads to product paralysis, where there's very little actual progress because direction is shifting too frequently. This is one of the top reasons apps fail to launch timely."[2]

~Nneka Ukpai, Investor, Philanthropist, and Tech executive

Design Handoff

You may recall from the design chapter that apps start as wireframes, are streamlined into a high-fidelity mockup, and then are converted into a prototype—a design with colors, photos, and elements that will give you the feel of what the product will look like in use. Your prototype, along with the feedback you get surrounding it, should prove whether the user flow you designed a few chapters ago actually made sense.

After a prototype is completed, designers will facilitate a *design handoff*, which is the process of providing a finished design to a development team for implementation. In preparation for this, the designer will bundle their design library—a package of commonly reusable design elements, components, and styles and the rules of their usage—and transfer them to the technical team to start building the architecture of the app.

PROVIDING DESIGN FEEDBACK

Before and during design handoff, it's important to strike a balance between confidence in your current designs and flexibility for future changes. Remember, this is just your MVP, so prioritize your must-haves to avoid endless iterations. While you can make changes to your designs later in the development process, be aware that this will cause you to incur additional hours and redesign and development fees beyond the original quoted scope. Although you can't predict every future change request, you can minimize them by providing design feedback to your team as early as possible in the process.

APPRENEUR INSIGHT

On prioritizing design during product development . . .

"What most first-time nontechnical founders fail to realize is that, for the most part, design teams only do what they are told. They are contractors. They get a job, review the specs and try to deliver as close to spec as possible with built-in review processes for iteration prior to pushing to dev. With this being said, if instructions are vague or designs are incomplete and left for interpretation, that is exactly what will happen. When things are left for interpretation, dev teams are like any other contractor; they will typically complete the project to the best of their understanding and at the lowest cost to their firm. An example is, if you provide a builder with designs for your kitchen remodel and just list 'countertops' with no specifics, you are going to receive standard countertops because it's the easiest for the builder to source and is the lowest cost, which provides more profit margins for them. You need to specifically state 'granite countertops' if that is your expectation. It is no different when working with a development team; specificity is key."[3]

~Chris Davis, CEO at Fansub

Your team will likely upload your designs to a design tool like Figma or Helio to share their work. These platforms enable you to leave direct feedback directly on different components of each design and discuss it with the team in real time.

Ahead of the handoff, follow these three steps to ensure that you provide comprehensive feedback for your design renderings:

1. Review each design rendering individually to ensure it is what you envisioned.

   Evaluate for the following:

- *Brand alignment:* Is the design aesthetically pleasing? Does it meet the guidelines set in your brand kit?

- *Objectivity:* Does this design serve its intended purpose? Will this design allow you to implement your business model?
- *Usability:* Is the design readable and error-free, and does it seem like it will work well across each of your mobile device platforms? Your design tool will likely allow you to see how each page will be displayed on each device.

2. Leave comments directly on or near the design with clear and precise feedback, suggestions, and change requests. Feel free to attach any photos, templates, or examples that may help your team better visualize your annotations and any changes you'd like to see. If you're not using a design tool, organize all your notes in order by the number or labeling of each rendering.
3. Once your dev team has had a chance to review the comments, coordinate a brief call to discuss. Use this as an opportunity for you to give the team more clarity and a better understanding of your feedback and requests.

Implementation

As discussed in earlier lessons, the development process is typically divided into three integral parts: the front end, the back end, and the APIs.

Again, the front end is the user interface of your app, or the portion that your end users will touch, feel, and experience. The back end is the database that supports the functions of your app; it connects to systems, stores information, and is responsible for performance and security. The back end fulfills requests from the front end, like when a user presses a button or fills out a form, and ultimately it establishes what your app can and can't do. An *application programming interface (API)* is a set of communication protocols for implementing software together.[4] APIs help to connect tools so they can add new features or functionality to your app.

The front and back end have a bit of a chicken-egg problem and there's quite a bit of debate surrounding which should get built first. Design-centric teams will argue for the front end, while developers will often push for the back. It can vary based on what's being built, the framework it's being built on, team strengths, or even constraints. But ultimately, if your team is large enough, it's perfectly fine to develop them both in tandem. In the event a change needs to be made, building them in parallel will allow you the flexibility to quickly alter one or the other.

Your development team will be building your app across a *software development cycle, which is a* workflow that defines the core stages and activities of the development process.[5] There are many different models and methodologies they can use to execute the cycle, each with a slightly different approach to completing the stages of app development.

Three of the most popular models in mobile development are waterfall, scrum, and agile.

- *Waterfall:* The waterfall method follows a step-by-step process, starting with a requirements analysis and ending with maintenance. Think of it as a master plan that trickles down in a very rigid, systematic way. It is known to work well for development projects that have very concrete and precise requirements.

WATERFALL

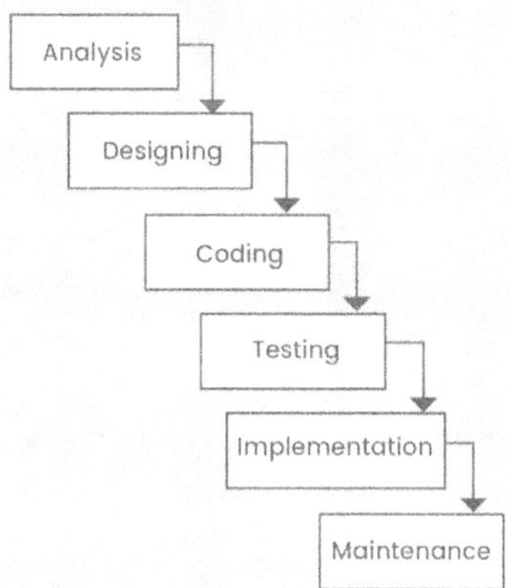

- *Agile:* For projects with more nuances and complexities, an agile method is generally preferred.[6] This approach favors responding to change as it happens versus maintaining strict plans. It breaks down projects into multiple cycles and focuses on the team's ability to continuously collaborate with the client over those cycles of feedback and iteration to get the project done.

AGILE CHART

TEST
DEPLOY
DEVELOP
REVIEW
DESIGN
REQUIREMENTS

- *Scrum:* Scrum is a form of agile project management framework characterized by ongoing collaboration across timed development cycles called *sprints*, during which specific work must be completed and made ready for review.[7]

SCRUM

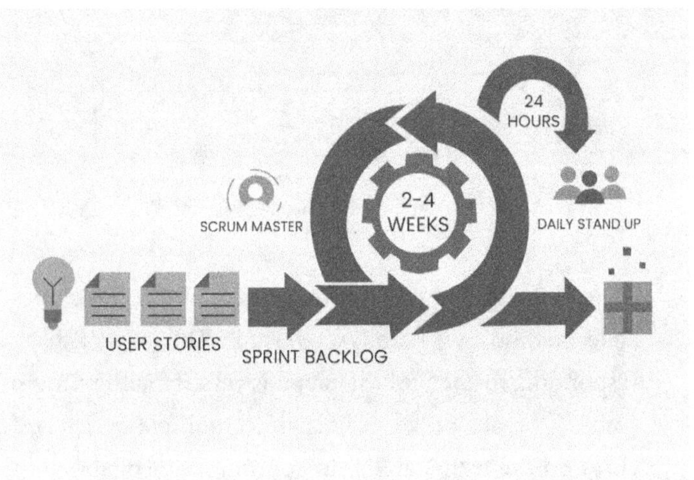

Teams using the scrum method are known to have regular checkpoints, including the following:

- *Planning meetings: Sessions to identify the team's key priorities of each sprint.*
- *Commitment meetings: During these meetings, teams will review their backlog of work to see how much time and effort they need to dedicate to completing it and what needs to be done in the upcoming sprint.*
- *Daily stand-ups: Short check-ins to communicate updates, blockers, or concerns and make sure the team is in alignment.*

- *Demos: Product demonstrations with the client, to show features and functionalities implemented during the current sprint.*
- *Retrospectives: Review meetings at the end of each sprint to discuss key learnings, what went well, and what needs to be improved moving forward.*

Before a sprint, developers review the client's requirements and convert them into user stories, which shifts the focus from writing about these deliverables to talking about them. The team then decides what items can be completed across one sprint, which typically lasts between two weeks to one month. Developers often set up a tool called a *Kanban board* to organize who on their team should be working on what and to visually track their progress.[8] The board contains several columns, including the following:

- *Backlog:* New client requests and product bugs
- *The next sprint:* Tasks that are scheduled to be worked on next
- *To-do list:* What's currently in progress
- *Testing:* Items currently being tested
- *Done:* Requirements that have been completed

Depending on the team's needs, developers may also include these optional columns:

- *Blocked:* Tasks that are stuck and cannot proceed due to unresolved issues
- *On Hold:* Tasks temporarily paused
- *Next Up:* High-priority tasks queued for immediate action after the current work is completed

- *Peer Review:* Tasks that require evaluation or feedback from team members before moving forward
- *Archived:* Tasks that are completed, canceled, or no longer relevant, yet stored for reference

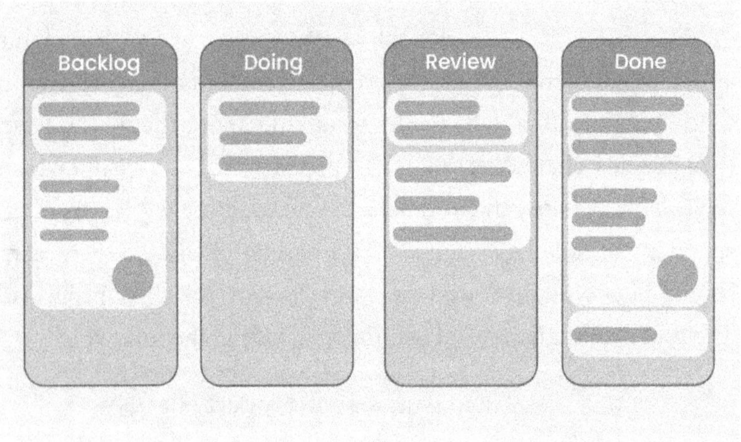

The requirements can float in and out of these categories, as sometimes a project needs more work, to go back to *in progress*, or needs to be retested.

"Why do I need to know this, Amanda?"

The internal model your dev team uses may influence your client experience. A team using the scrum methodology may request far more meetings or client interactions than one implementing the waterfall process. Neither is better or worse; it's just a matter of perspective and using the best framework for the product you're building.

Regardless of the model they use, there are a few common practices during development that all app entrepreneurs must anticipate:

- *Weekly to bi-weekly meetings and updates:* Whether it's by email, messaging, or video chat, you may receive updates and be required to attend meetings on a regular basis.
- *Project management dashboard:* Your team may invite you to a project management dashboard where you can see the progress track of your project in real time. You may have another project management tool you prefer, but in my opinion, it is always better to allow your dev team to use the one they are most comfortable with. You want them to focus on your app, not the learning curve of an unfamiliar platform.
- *Recurring testing and reviews:* You will need to participate in tests to ensure your team has accurately implemented or completed features.
- *Ongoing asset requests:* Outside of development, there is an array of supplementary material needed to bring an app to market. We will go over a comprehensive list of these assets in the next chapter.
- *Payment milestones:* Depending on your arrangement, you will make payments as sprints or milestones are completed.

Building an app is a commitment of your time, money, and effort. To see this project to completion, you will need to not only be present but also be an advocate for yourself. If any of the foregoing items are not happening, be proactive about requesting that they do. Don't be afraid to put time on your team's calendar to make sure the app works as intended. Again, as the client, *you* have the power here.

DEVELOPER INSIGHT

"I wish clients, generally speaking, were more aware of the effort required on their side to have a good software outsourcing relationship. It's easy to fall into the trap of assuming that once you outsource, you've delegated all responsibilities and your job is done. However, that isn't the case. At the end of the day, a client knows their business better than anyone else (or at least should!). A developer, someone contracted to work on a project that they don't have any previous knowledge of, needs the continuous insight and direction from the visionary (client) to properly guide their work and reduce the number of assumptions that need to be made. Assumptions are the Achilles's heel of any outsourcing project.

~David Pawlan, Co-Founder at Aloa.[9]

During this phase, you'll be introduced to a number of new terms. A few of the most common are as follows:

- *Hosting*

  Hosting. Many mobile apps need network access, or to be "hosted" somewhere for users to download and use them. Hosting involves running your application on someone else's infrastructure, allowing the app to be available from a third-party server or a cloud service accessed via the internet.

Not all apps require hosting. Some are designed as standalone solutions that can be launched independently from a user's phone, tablet, or browser. However, if your app needs to pull information or store data on the back end, you will likely need a hosting service provider for full-feature availability.

If your app requires hosting, your development team will notify you. Once you choose a service provider and open an account, your team will connect your app's code, databases, and necessary components and upload them to the platform (or server), making the app accessible to anyone who installs or accesses it via the web.

- *Database*

  Databases are mobile networks that allow you to share, store, modify, and delete data.

  There are two primary types of databases: SQL and NoSQL. Each of these options stores data, but they do it in different ways. Deciding which database type to use depends heavily on the type of information you're storing and how you'll be utilizing it.

  If your data is highly structured and you don't anticipate much change in the data, then SQL is probably the best choice. But if you anticipate a large influx in traffic or data usage, you may want to opt for NoSQL, which, with its use of cloud infrastructure, is better aligned for growth. Refer to your developer for advice on the best option for you.

- *Mobile analytics*

  Mobile analytics capture data from your app or website to

track, measure, record, and identify how mobile users are interacting with the app.

As your app is being developed, you'll want to ensure your developer integrates the analytics to give you more insights into how to grow, scale, and improve your app based on existing use.

- *Alpha testing*

  As your team begins to build, they will need to continually test the app from end to end to ensure it adequately meets your business and functional requirements. This process is called *alpha testing.* All these tests are performed by your developers internally in staged environments, and quality assurance leads to identifying major bugs and feature flaws ahead of making the product public.

  And there you have it—development in a nutshell. Not so bad, right? Complete this chapter's brief but essential checklist, and then move on to the next chapter, where you'll find a list of deliverables to address as your development team builds.

CHAPTER 11

Creating Your App's Assets

Just because you've handed your project over to a developer doesn't mean your work as a founder stops. You need to be regularly available during this time to communicate with and support your dev team, and you will also need to start creating your app's assets and begin positioning yourself to promote your app.

APPRENEUR INSIGHT

"Founders should spend this time generating sales and talking with prospective customers. Even if the product is not finished, you can get bookings early by using mockups or developing the relationship with the customer."

~Jasmine Shells, Founder and CEO at Five to Nine [1]

Legal Assets

Let's start with the legal documents required for listing an app in the App or Play Store,[2] beginning with the terms and conditions and privacy policy.

Terms and Conditions

A terms and conditions (T&C) agreement, which can also be called ToS (terms of service) or ToU (terms of use), is an agreement between a business and a customer that sets rules for the user to follow and dictates how they may use your app. It details how users should behave on the app and what they should anticipate from you as the business in return. Inside the terms you'll include the following stipulations and information:

- The rules that users must follow
- What you as an app-based business are and are not responsible for
- Penalties for misusing the app, including account deletion
- Your copyright information
- Payment and subscription information, if relevant

There are many online tools that can provide you with a T&C template or enable you to customize your own. If you have access to a start-up attorney, they can help you draft a document as well.

Privacy Policy

In most countries, it is legally required for a business to disclose its privacy and data processing activities. Privacy policies are the legal statements that detail how a mobile app gathers, stores, and uses the personally identifiable information it collects from users. These policies must be clear and conspicuous and require each user's consent.

Your privacy policy should address the collection of all personal and sensitive information, including but not limited to the following items:

- Payment information
- Authentication information
- Location information
- Contacts, call, or SMS information
- Microphone or camera data
- Device or app usage data

Your app's privacy policy will need to cover the following:

- The forms of personal info you collect
- How the information is being collected
- Ways users can request details on the information being collected
- How you intend to use their personal information
- Any third parties you may grant access to or who may collect information from your website or app

Your policies will need to be visible in your app, on your website, and in your app store listing.

Depending on the nature of your app, you may require additional policies and statements such as a cookies and consent form, a return and refund policy, or a disclaimer. Consult with an attorney to determine exactly what you need to operate.

Brand Assets

If you completed the wireframe and app design activities, you may have already started thinking through your visual brand assets, but in the event you didn't, you'll want to start by consulting a graphic designer to make a brand identity kit (brand kit).

Brand kits are playbooks for the visual identity of your brand; they set guidelines to ensure aesthetic continuity across all assets.

Include the following items in your brand kits:

- *A logo*
- *Logo lockups:* Guidelines for how your logo can be used or displayed
- *Color palettes:* Each color in your scheme should include its corresponding *hex color code* (hex codes are a way of representing specific shades of color through hexadecimal values)
- *Typography and fonts*
- *Illustrative elements* (if applicable)

Collectively, these assets will be used as a benchmark to influence the way your app looks and feels across the app itself—as well as embassies like your website and social media pages—and the required collateral you'll need for uploading your app to the store.

App Store Assets

As a part of your submission process to the App or Play Store you'll be required to create and upload metadata with your app. Metadata is the collection of brand assets, links, and information that describes your app and will be displayed to users on your store listing. These elements provide an opportunity to magnify your app's value and cut through the clutter of competition with visuals and information that detail why a user should download your product.

App Name

Let's start with your app name. In both the App and Play Stores you have a limit of thirty characters to name your app. If you have the space, include a short keyword-infused description of the app. This will help to articulate what you do and boost your listing during user search.

- Your name should be simple and easy to understand.
- Do not include common app titles, special characters, prices, celebrity names, or any trademarked/protected words in your title.

App Icon

Your icon will be the image users recognize you by in the app stores and on their devices. Your icon should be visually and aesthetically focused—so as tempting as it may be, avoid heavy text in the image.

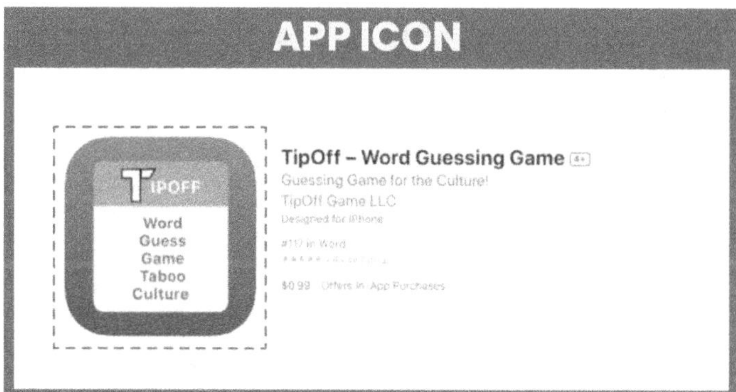

Examples of the CultureCrush Icon over the Years

Subtitle

Your subtitle should complement your name and icon. Similar to your app name, you'll have thirty characters in the Apple App Store and fifty characters in Google Play to provide a short synopsis of the benefits of your app. This text should entice visitors to click on the app's icon to learn more.

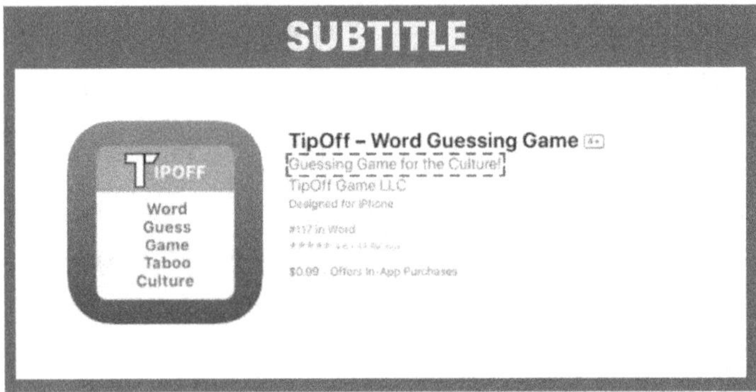

Your subtitle adds a little razzle-dazzle to your app's name and description.

Screenshots

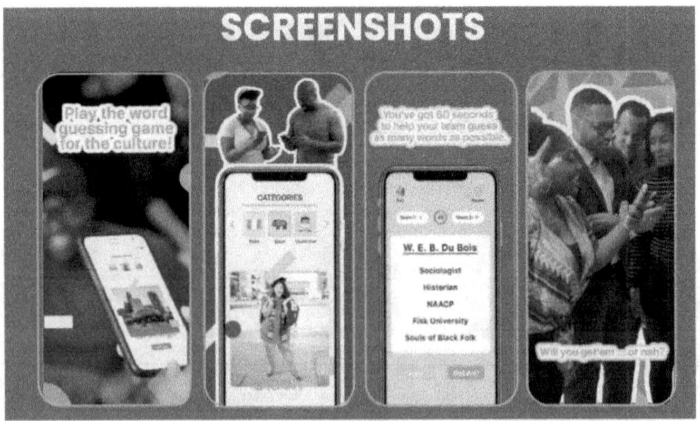

Screenshots for TipOff—Word Guessing Game

Your screenshots give a glimpse of what the app looks like and also give you the opportunity to tell a visual story about how the app can be used and the experience users will have once they've downloaded. Your screenshots must be an accurate representation of the app itself, so you may want to work with your developers or on-team designer(s) to strategize about these images.

Screenshots are displayed vertically in the Apple App Store and both vertically and horizontally in Google Play. Each store has its own dimensions and parameters for submission. A comprehensive guide of app store dimension sizes can be found inside our community, The App Accelerator.

What's New?

Found exclusively on the Apple App Store, the "What's New" section is an outlet for app owners to share updates and information with their users. From new features to add-ons, this space can be a fun and interesting way to keep users in the loop about what's new, now, and next with your product.

Promotional Text

Also only on Apple, promotional text is like the "What's New" section but with a focus on time-sensitive promotional announcements. Use this corner of the page to highlight your app's promotional activities, including giveaways or limited-time experiences.

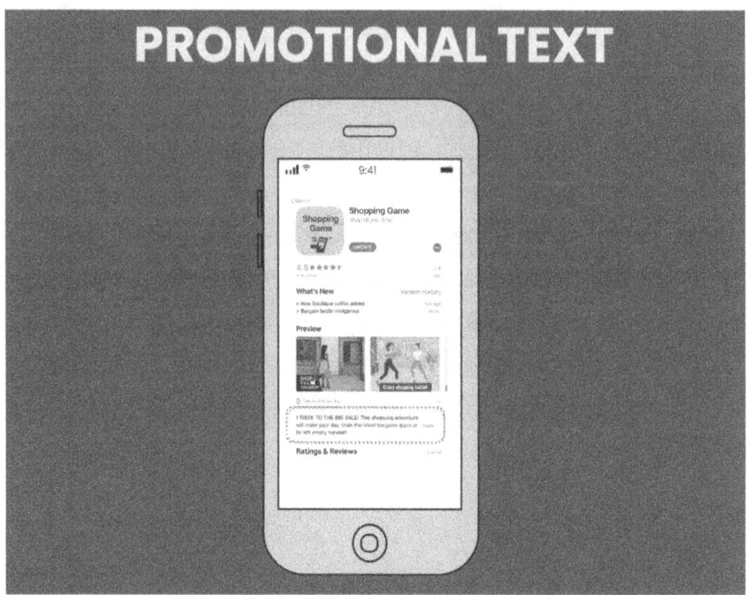

Description

The description section of your listing is a long-form text box where you can share content about your app's purpose, features, and benefits. Both Apple and Google Play provide a 4,000-character limit you can fill with keywords to make your listing more search-friendly and visible in your category.

- Google Play offers two description sections: the 4,000-character section mentioned above, as well as a shorter 80-character description.
- The first three lines (170 characters) of the App Store description display above the fold of the page, making it one of the first things a user sees. Think through these words carefully to give users the best first impression of your app.

Keywords

We briefly touched on keywords earlier in the book, but as a refresher, these are descriptive words, terms, and phrases users will type into search to find an app like yours. Both stores provide a 100-character section where you can list the words most closely aligned with your app. To increase your visibility in the app stores, use these words in the description section and repeat them throughout your listing.

Preview Video

In the App Store, you can include one to three short videos alongside your screenshots. The videos auto-play on mute and can last up to thirty seconds. You can use this space to give a video preview of the app itself or insert a fun, creative concept. App preview videos can be localized—translated into different languages in each respective country.

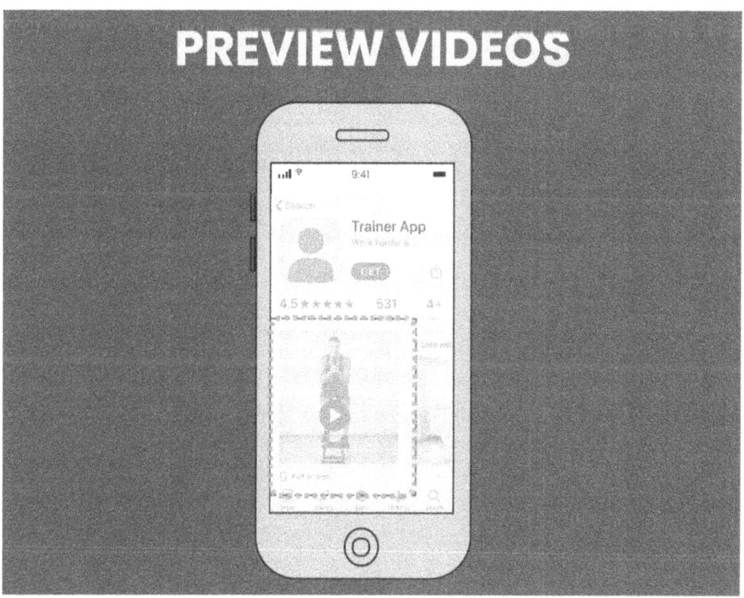

Promotional Video

The equivalent of the preview video on Google Play is called the promotional video and while it serves the same purpose, there are a few distinct differences. Google Play only allows room for one promotional video, but it will be displayed as a horizontal header across your listing. The video does not auto-play (as it will need to be a YouTube video), and it will not be listed with your screenshot in Play Store search results.

Support URLs

In addition to your terms of use and privacy policy, you will need a support URL to submit your app to either store. This link provides users with an outlet to contact you directly from your listing. Most people list their website's contact page.

Marketing URL

Your marketing link is a website URL that leads to additional details about your app. Generally, app founders route this link to their homepage or a landing page (a site specifically dedicated to the app where users can download the app, join a mailing list, or find out more information).

Categories

Apps in both stores are listed by categories. You are allowed to select a primary and secondary category. The secondary category is often a subcategory of the primary.

With our game TipOff, we selected "Games" as our primary category and "Word Guessing" as our secondary category.

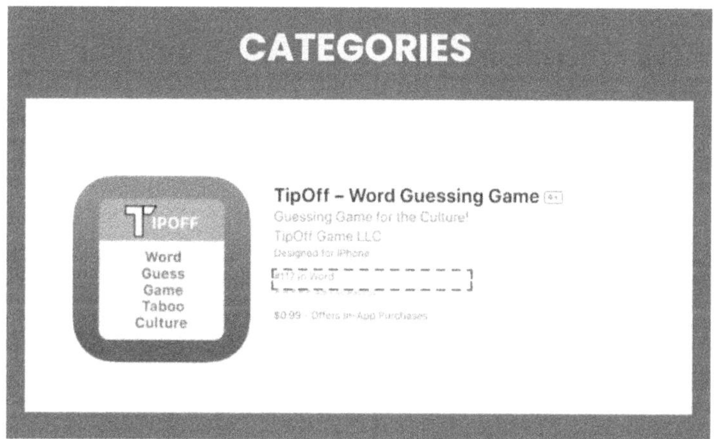

TipOff frequently ranks in the top of the word guessing subcategory.

Select the categories that tie most closely to the core functionality of your app, as well as the bucket where you think prospective users will look for it.

STORE CATEGORIES

Apple App store Categories	App store Game subcategories	Google Play categories	Google Play Game
Books	*Action*	Art & Design	*Action*
Business	*Adventure*	Auto & Vehicles	*Adventure*
Developer tools	*Arcade*	Beauty	*Arcade*
Education	*Board*	Books & Reference	*Board*
Entertainment	*Card*	Business	*Card*
Finance	*Casino*	Communication	*Casino*
Food & Drink	*Family*	Dating	*Educational*
Games	*Music*	Education	*Music*
Grapihics & Design	*Puzzle*	Entertainment	*Puzzle*
Health & Fitness	*Role Playing*	Events	*Racing*
Lifestyle	*Simulation*	Food & Drink	*Role Playing*
Kids (iOS & iPad OS only)	*Sports*	Health & Fitness	*Simulation*
Magazines & Newsapers	*Strategy*	House & Home	*Sports*
Medical	*Trivia*	Libraries & Demo	*Strategy*
Music	*Word*	Lifestyle	*Trivia*
Navigation		Maps and navigation	*Word*

Demo Account

While the demo account won't be visible to the public, it is a critically important component of getting and keeping your app in either store. When you submit your app to a store, it goes through a review process to ensure you meet all store guidelines. If your app has a login process, it is always helpful to provide the reviewer with a demo or test login to give them easy access to your content and eliminate all potential barriers to entry. If a reviewer can't log in to your app for any given reason, the app's submission will be rejected, and you will be required to either send the reviewer detailed notes or restart the submission process altogether. Trust me, I've learned this one the hard way.

In-App Purchases

If you have in-app purchases within your app, this feature is where you provide information about these assorted upgrades. For each in-app purchase, you are allocated a short title and description text box where you can provide users with a short synopsis of what's included with the purchase.

Use this section to describe what is available for sale in your app.

Additional Tasks and Responsibilities

Outside of producing your assets, you should be preparing to sell the product to come. Use this time to start getting yourself into the rhythm of app ownership. Here are a few best practices for making the most of this time:

- *Team check-ins*: Create a cadence of weekly standups and conference calls with your development and business team.
- *Continued customer discovery:* App development is a never-ending learning process. Meet with as many people as possible in your target audience to collect additional product or marketing insights.
- *Create a waitlist:* Ideally, you want to launch your app to a list of eager and excited users. Refer to the brand audit we did earlier in the book to secure the right website domain and set up a landing page for users to sign up.
- *Sell, sell, SELL:* If possible, pre-sell your app and its services with a soft pitch to potential partners and customers. Depending on the nature of your business, some companies may be willing to sign *letters of intent* (LOIs) or *memorandums of understanding* (MOUs), which are non-legally-binding agreements that outline an agreement to work together before a final, formal contract is produced.

Even if clients don't immediately sign on the dotted line, self-promotion not only sharpens your sales skills but is also a great way to grow your waitlist and build momentum ahead of launch.

APPRENEUR INSIGHT

On how founders should be using their time during development . . .

"User research, raising capital, talking to as many people as possible. Likely, at this stage, you won't have a ton of 'admin' work, but make sure your house is in order. You can never have too much customer feedback."[3]

~Matthew Hall, Sports Investor and Entrepreneur

Chapter checklist

- ☐ Draft your T&C.
- ☐ Draft your privacy policy.
- ☐ Craft your brand identity kit.
- ☐ Determine app store name.
- ☐ Create app store icon.
- ☐ Determine app store subtitle.
- ☐ Design app store screenshots.
- ☐ Draft your app store description.
- ☐ Determine your app store keywords.
- ☐ Identify your support URL.
- ☐ Identify your marketing URL.
- ☐ Select your app store categories.
- ☐ Create a demo account.
- ☐ Make a list of your in-app purchases.

CHAPTER 12

Testing Your App

Have you ever read the description for a tool or service, gotten all excited to use it, and paid your money only to find out it didn't work? The worst!

Now imagine being a potential user, eager to use this problem-solving, cutting-edge app, only to leave out of disappointment and frustration when it doesn't work—never to return again.

This doesn't have to be you and your business. The key to preventing this experience is thorough testing. Testing guarantees that a product meets your expectations and functions as intended before it ever reaches your customers' hands.

As we discussed in chapter 10, testing comes in many different forms but should always start internally with your dev team during the alpha phase. Alpha testing is the crucial preliminary step that acts as the gateway to ensuring your app is thoroughly vetted and most prepared for the app stores. This process helps catch major issues early, paving the way for a more polished and reliable final product for the public. Some of the most common alpha tests include the following:

- *Functional testing:* This test checks key features to determine if they work as described in the requirements.
- *Usability testing:* Your designer should strive to ensure that features are intuitive and user-friendly and that no part of the app is cumbersome, clunky, or confusing.
- *Performance testing:* This test focuses on how fast the app loads and its responsiveness on mobile devices. An app could be fully functional, but if it loads slowly, a user will assume it's broken.
- *Fit and finish testing:* A design-centric test, this review process determines whether the developed features match the original, approved designs.
- *Regression testing:* Regression testing involves testing the features created in previous sprints. As updates are made throughout the app, you must continually test all features to ensure they still work as intended.
- *Device-specific testing:* This test is meant to check the app across different device types, models, and sizes.

Many of these tests may happen more informally as you build, but one form of testing that should always be thoughtfully prescheduled in a controlled environment is your *beta test.*

Beta Tests

Beta testing is a form of user acceptance testing that determines if an app meets the specified requirements and is ready for release. These tests are moderated by you as the entrepreneur, alongside your development team, in a live environment. They are conducted with potential and prospective users—also known as early adopters—who provide direct feedback on the product. Beta tests are considered the final tests before making the product widely available to customers and the public.

These tests help detect bugs, ensure quality, and make sure the integrity of the app is upheld across devices. Beta tests can also be a great marketing tactic to build anticipation for the upcoming product release, making beta testing ideal to begin the final leg of the iD3 framework: deployment. Note that some developers consider beta testing as much a part of the development phase as of the building of the app itself.

Types of Beta Tests

Beta tests can typically be classified into open or closed tests.

Closed tests, or *private beta,* is when the testing is limited to a group of selected and invited people who may be current customers, early adopters, or even focus groups. They typically come ahead of open testing.

In an *open test,* or *public beta*, the app is released to the market, and anyone can evaluate the product and provide relevant feedback and reviews. If you opt for an open beta test, it's helpful to let users know the status of the app with some form of in-app messaging or in your app description. Letting users know that you're in beta can make users feel special—not only as early adopters of the product but as a part of your journey as you grow and scale the platform.

If your app has a lot of buzz or anticipation around its release, you may want to consider an *early access release*. Popularized by gaming apps, early access release involves users paying to test an incomplete version of software to fund development and provide feedback that may influence the final product. If you have an existing following, this may be a great option for eager and excited users to get early access to the app before the general public, while you and your team can continue to conduct technical and usability tests.

How to Conduct a Beta Test

At the root of it, beta tests are simply an opportunity for you to collect feedback on your product. However, because this will likely be a user's first time interacting with your app, you'll need to take additional steps to ensure that the engagement is focused and streamlined and garners the insights you need to make necessary improvements. Use the following instructions to prepare for your first beta test.

STEP 1: FINALIZE ALL FEATURES

First, ensure all your final must-have features are available and visible in the app. If anything is still in development, consider postponing the test if possible or having your developers gate (block access to) that part of the app to avoid distractions. Much of your success in beta testing involves creating a fixed and controlled environment for testers to analyze; you don't want to inadvertently impact your results by overwhelming or confusing your testers with a partially done product.

STEP 2: SET YOUR TESTING OBJECTIVES

Next, you'll want to set structured testing objectives. Similar in style to the requirements you set for your app, beta testing objectives outline the features and functionalities you would like to test. Beta testing objectives can typically be split into primary and secondary categories.

Your primary objective is the main outcome you want to measure or achieve, answering whether this app solves the problem in the way it was intended to? For example:

To assess whether ScanURfilez app effectively enables users to convert photos of documents into scanned PDFs.

Secondary objectives are other elements being reviewed during the test that either give more context to the findings from the primary objective or give insights about how users feel about those additional elements and features. To continue our example:

Secondary Objective 1: To evaluate whether users understand the instructions given in the ScanUrfilez "How it works" section.

Secondary Objective 2: To ensure that there are no broken buttons or links throughout the app.

Brainstorm all the user-facing functions in the app and then write testing objectives surrounding them.

How many questions should you ask your testers?

Ask your testers enough questions to cover your objectives but not so many that users start to feel exhausted or overwhelmed.

Strive to have a mix of fixed responses (yes/no) and others that are open-ended. You'll want to keep things fluid enough so testers feel comfortable sharing their thoughts, feelings, and even criticisms with you. Encourage them to think out loud and voice the first things that come to mind.

STEP 3: SELECT TESTING TOOLS

Next, you'll need to select your testing tools and platforms.

Users will already have a learning curve onboarding to your app; you don't want to make onboarding any more difficult than it has to be. Testing tools will enable you to easily deploy the app to your users and gain their insights without making the app fully available to the public.

Many appreneurs opt to use Google Play's Beta Program or Apple's TestFlight to conduct beta tests. However, there are several different tools and platforms you can use. When you're deciding which tool is right for you, consider the following factors:

- *Platforms:* Is it only available for iOS? Android? Cross-platform?
- *Ease of use:* If there is a fifteen-step sign-up process, your users will likely check out mentally before they even get to download the product.
- *Cost:* Some testing platforms are free, while others come with a cost.
- *Set-up time:* Your time is as valuable as your users'; search for how-to onboarding videos to get started quickly.
- *Bug reporting:* Can testers report bugs and incidents inside the tool or will you need an additional method of collecting feedback?

Once you find the testing platform, familiarize yourself with it by onboarding yourself and downloading your own app. As you do, take the initiative to outline the tool's onboarding instructions for your testing participants—sometimes these will be provided by the platform, but sometimes you'll need to draft them yourself. There's a great chance that your testing participants won't be familiar with your testing platform, so having these instructions handy will make for an easier transition, especially when tests are being facilitated remotely.

STEP 4: RECRUIT PARTICIPANTS

Ideally, your tester groups should consist of members of your target persona. If all goes well, these testers will be your future evangelists, so you'll want people who are invested in the problem and excited to see you solve it. You'll find it easier to attract testers if you ask for their feedback in exchange for something of value. Cash incentives and gift cards typically work well, but if you're not quite there yet, early or complimentary access to your platform may suffice.

If you can't confirm whether someone is in your core audience, you may need to prescreen them with a brief survey or questionnaire. When screening, try to avoid yes or no questions, as people tend to bend the truth in order to get the perks and incentives. Your screening questions shouldn't disclose any information about the desired answer; instead, give several viable options that could all be possibilities. Candidates won't know what you're looking for in a tester unless you tell them.

If applicable, start searching for testers within your social network. Although putting yourself out there can be scary, there are likely more people than you realize willing to support your venture. In addition to a personal post, you can also search platforms like Twitter, Facebook, or Instagram using hashtags like #BetaTesting or #TestMyApp to find people who enjoy offering feedback.

If you're not finding much success with your personal network, there are beta testing and user recruitment platforms where you'll find communities of eager testers. Quora and Reddit communities can also be a great place to share news and post content about new and emerging apps. Some marketers even suggest recruiting testers from your competitors!

How many testers will I need?

As discouraging as it sounds, if the test is done remotely or in the user's spare time, there's a good chance that many of your testers won't complete their surveys. Sometimes people get busy with life, some lose interest, and others simply don't have much feedback to contribute.

All things considered, you should attempt to determine the number of people you'll need to reach a learning plateau and then double or triple it. The key is to have a large enough group that you can get enough actionable insights but not so many that you can't monitor responses in an efficient manner.

STEP 5: DISTRIBUTE BETA AGREEMENTS

Once you find your core group of test participants, you'll need them to sign participant agreements to establish guidelines for testing and protect your intellectual property. A *beta agreement* (also known as a beta test software agreement, beta policy, beta license agreement, or beta participant agreement form) lays out the relationship, terms, and policies between your company and your testers. While these agreements mostly focus on terms like how long a test might last or the powers held by each party, there may also be a nondisclosure or confidentiality agreement within the contract.

Contracts and agreements can sound scary and intimidating, but they don't have to be in practice. When you're recruiting testers, simply create a short contact form for all interested parties to register through. The beta agreement can be listed as a statement next to a checkbox on your form, which users can acknowledge and consent to with one click.

STEP 6: ONBOARD THE TESTERS

Ahead of the test, you'll need to set testing parameters and provide the testers with a brief instructional overview that outlines your ask of them and what they can anticipate from this experience.

Include the following information in your overview:

- *Description:* A one-sentence description of your app will suffice.

- *Test environment and expectations:* Detailed information surrounding the time commitment and what is expected of them in the test. Will you be testing in a group? Staging one-on-one tests? Will testers be remote? What can testers anticipate?
- *Incentives:* If you can compensate your testers for their time and effort with a gift card, cash, or even pizza—please do so.
- *Prerequisites*: Are there requirements testers need to meet or complete before being accepted into the test group?
- *Call to action:* Tell people what they should do next. For example, if you'd like your testers to click a link to complete a registration form and then download the testing tool, you'll need to detail this in the message and provide the corresponding link or assets they need to proceed.

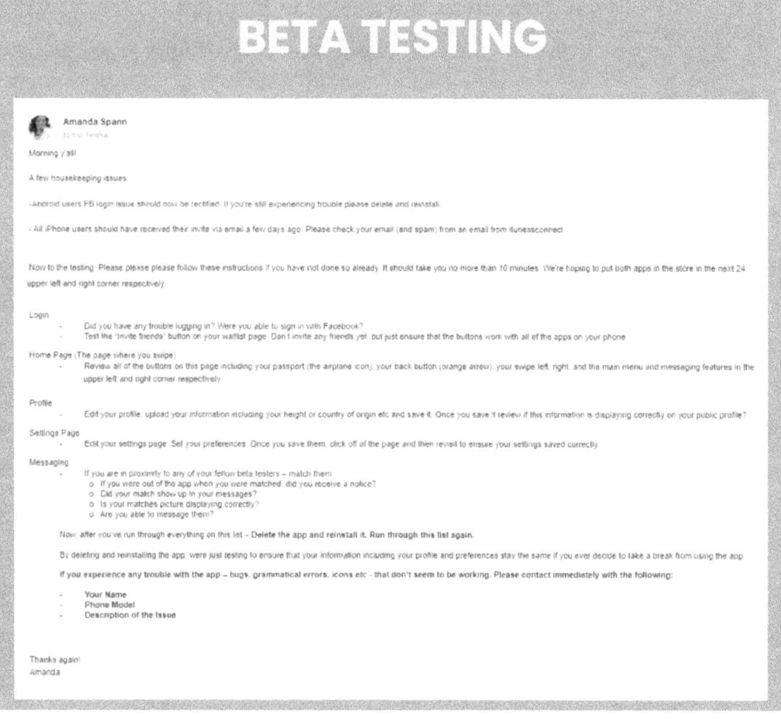

BETA TESTING

Amanda Spann

Morning y'all!

A few housekeeping issues

-Android users FB login issue should now be rectified. If you're still experiencing trouble please delete and reinstall.

- All iPhone users should have received their invite via email a few days ago. Please check your email (and spam) from an email from itunesconnect

Now to the testing. Please please please follow these instructions if you have not done so already. It should take you no more than 10 minutes. We're hoping to put both apps in the store in the next 24 upper left and right corner respectively

Login
- Did you have any trouble logging in? Were you able to sign in with Facebook?
- Test the "invite friends" button on your waitlist page. Don't invite any friends yet, but just ensure that the buttons work with all of the apps on your phone

Home Page (The page where you swipe)
- Review all of the buttons on this page including your passport (the airplane icon), your back button (orange arrow), your swipe left, right, and the main menu and messaging features in the upper left and right corner respectively

Profile
- Edit your profile, upload your information including your height or country of origin etc and save it. Once you save it review if this information is displaying correctly on your public profile?

Settings Page
- Edit your settings page. Set your preferences. Once you save them, click off of the page and then revisit to ensure your settings saved correctly

Messaging
- If you are in proximity to any of your fellow beta testers – match them
  - If you were out of the app when you were matched, did you receive a notice?
  - Did your match show up in your messages?
  - Is your matches picture displaying correctly?
  - Are you able to message them?

Now, after you've run through everything on this list – **Delete the app and reinstall it. Run through this list again.**

By deleting and reinstalling the app, were just testing to ensure that your information including your profile and preferences stay the same if you ever decide to take a break from using the app

If you experience any trouble with the app – bugs, grammatical errors, icons etc - that don't seem to be working. Please contact immediately with the following:

- **Your Name**
- **Phone Model**
- **Description of the Issue**

Thanks again!
Amanda

How long should the test take?

The length of your test will be contingent upon several factors, like the nature of your app, the objectives you set, and your resources, as well as testing limitations.

Perhaps you think a fixed-timed focus group would be most appropriate for your audience, or maybe giving the users free rein to experiment with the app over a few hours or days feels like a better fit. Construct the test you think will give you the insights you need to make improvements, but be mindful of distractions. Collecting feedback is *your top priority; your testers may not necessarily feel the same way. You'll want to be sure to keep them on track and follow up with them as often as required.*

Historically, most of my beta testing experiences have taken a minimum of two weeks from planning to execution, but they can easily run longer as you iterate and make improvements. Give yourself enough time to outline a thoughtful and data-driven test structure, conduct the test itself, and review and implement feedback.

STEP 7: CONDUCT TEST AND COLLECT INSIGHTS

It's safe to say that all beta tests will look slightly different. Regardless of the route you decide to take, there are a few best practices that will ensure you meet your objectives:

- *Keep questionnaires concise:* Brevity is important inside of your app as well as for any tool you may be using to collect feedback on it. Long, drawn-out forms often lead to app abandonment and incorrect data submissions from testers.
- *Remove your bias:* If at all possible, avoid interruptions and interjections. Be mindful of the ways you may accidentally insert your own bias into the process. Even something as

simple as agreeing with a user's comment or asking for confirmation of a particular opinion can sway testers to answer in a way they feel is favorable to you.

- *Ask for clarity:* Consider that some of your testers may not be very tech savvy, and even if they are, they may not be the best communicators. Most people will do their best to describe their issues or concerns, but others may struggle to articulate what they're thinking. Feel free to follow up post-test to ask for clarity on their feedback but be careful not to prompt them to respond one way or another.
- *Collect images, videos, and screenshots:* One of the biggest challenges developers face when fixing a reported bug is pinpointing and replicating the error. Users know when something is wrong with an app, but they rarely know how to describe what happened and the circumstances around it. Encourage testers to take screenshots or screen recordings any time they experience a bug. If they forget to take a screenshot, prompt them with relevant questions, for example, "What were you doing immediately before or after the error?" Aggregating supporting assets will make revising and improving the app a simpler process.

STEP 8: REVISE AND RETEST

After tests are conducted and the feedback has been submitted, take time to rewatch videos, review submissions, and consolidate all the suggestions, recommendations, and errors you received. Know that some of your testers will likely have some outlandish ideas or app-altering suggestions. Hear them out, but don't take anything to heart. Remember, you can't always be everything to everyone.

Feel free to revisit the MoSCoW prioritization method from chapter 8 to decide which items should be implemented as revisions to your app. Then summarize these action items to your development team and any other relevant team members. The bug fixes alone may take weeks or even months to rectify. Be patient with yourself and your team.

Outside of dissecting the data, this is also a good time to evaluate if your customer persona profiles are still valid or if you need to brainstorm new segments to recruit and research.

APPRENEUR INSIGHT

"It is important to always understand the problem looking to be solved behind a customer feature request. Customers provide solutions that they think will solve the root problem but at the end of the day, you are the expert. We definitely built things at times that didn't matter or weren't used, looking to fulfill a customer's request. Make sure to always ask and validate 'the why' behind every request."

~Jasmine Shells, Founder and CEO at Five to Nine[1]

Once all the changes are implemented, it may be helpful to retest with the same group of testers or a new group with fresh eyes. Collect insights on their reaction to the revisions or if they even notice the changes. Make a second round of edits if necessary.

STEP 9: COMMERCIAL RELEASE

Commercial release refers to the moment when your app becomes available to users who aren't just testers. This is the point when we begin to release your app to the App Store or Google Play.

Confirm your app's readiness for commercial release by checking off the following items:

- *Bug-free experience:* All major bugs and issues have been resolved.
- *Performance:* The app runs smoothly without crashes or significant slowdowns.
- *Security:* All security vulnerabilities, if any, have been addressed and fixed.
- *Usability:* The app is intuitive and easy to use for the target audience.
- *Feature completeness:* All planned features are fully implemented and functional.
- *Compatibility:* The app works across all intended devices and operating systems.
- *Compliance:* The app meets all regulatory and compliance requirements, as well as those of the app stores.
- *Scalability:* The app can handle the expected user load and traffic.

Outside of taking the first step, this part of the process is probably the scariest for most app entrepreneurs. We've spent countless hours tweaking, revising, and adding new elements to get to this point, and we want our app to be flawless when we make our big reveal to the world.

And while you want to strive for a bug-free app, you must be careful not to put yourself in revision purgatory. Your need for perfection can stand in the way of progress. Remember, it's okay to launch, iterate, and improve as you go!

Use the checklist to plan your beta test properly and prepare to take the next steps toward releasing your app publicly. In the next two chapters, we'll unpack your commercial release and publishing your app to the stores.

Chapter checklist

- [ ] Write testing objectives.
- [ ] Choose your testing platform.
- [ ] Outline onboarding instructions for each platform.
- [ ] Draft a beta agreement.
- [ ] Compose a registration form.
- [ ] Write a welcome email for testers.
- [ ] Oversee live tests.
- [ ] Itemize and prioritize feedback data.

CHAPTER 13

Submitting Your App to the App Store

Kudos to you for making it to the final stretch of your app development journey—deployment! By now your app should have been fully tested, making the process of uploading it to the Apple App Store and Google Play the last big step before your creation goes live. This is a significant milestone, and you should be proud of how far you've come.

This chapter will walk you step-by-step through the submission process, from preparing your app's assets to handling potential rejections, in the order that they will happen. We'll cover everything you need to ensure a smooth and successful launch. With detailed guidance, tips, and best practices, you'll navigate these final hurdles confidently.

It's a long chapter, but stick with me—you're almost at the finish line. Soon, your app will be available to millions of users, ready to make an impact. Let's dive in and do the work to make your launch a resounding success!

Earlier in the book, we briefly discussed the requirements and fees associated with enrolling in the Apple and Google Developer Programs. This chapter will detail the action items you need to perform within those accounts to submit your app and start processing and receiving payments. If you haven't yet created your accounts in those programs, please do that now.

We'll start first with the App Store. Despite Android making up 70 percent of the global smartphone market, developers often choose to release on the App Store first. This choice doesn't make Apple better or Google worse; it's a strategic decision. Since Android has multiple device types like Galaxy and Pixel, testing and releasing on iOS first helps developers streamline their review process. The uniformity of iOS across all Apple devices makes it easier to predict app behavior across various models, resulting in a more reliable rollout and the ability to identify and resolve potential issues earlier on all platforms.

Submitting Your App to Apple's App Store

You may not have realized it when you enrolled in the Apple Developer Program, but by creating this account, you automatically became the account holder for your membership. As the account holder, you have full admin privileges for all apps uploaded to the account and any associated agreements, banking information, users, and roles. You will manage these rights on the Apple Developer website and App Store Connect, a dashboard of web tools for managing and distributing apps on the App Store.

Accounts and Assigning Roles

If you enrolled in the Apple Developer program as an organization, you have the option of adding various members to your team.

The role you assign each team member gives them tiers of access to assorted development and distribution tools.

If you opted to enroll as an individual, you can still add team members on App Store Connect to help you manage the app. However, these users will not be considered part of your team in the Apple Developer Program.[1]

Roles

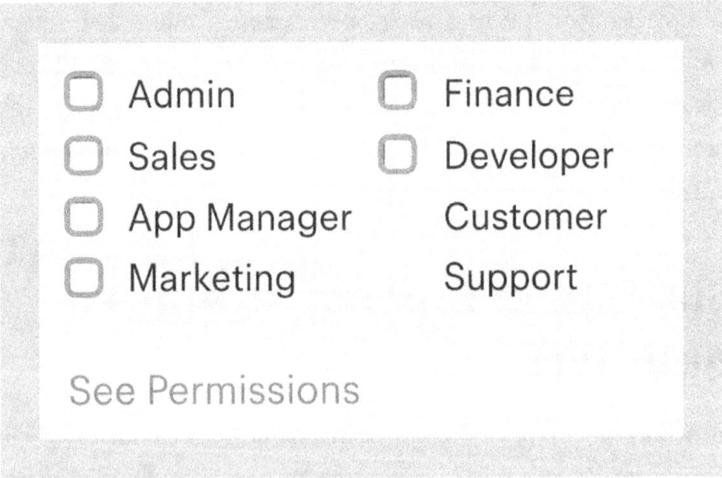

- ☐ Admin
- ☐ Sales
- ☐ App Manager
- ☐ Marketing
- ☐ Finance
- ☐ Developer
- Customer Support

See Permissions

Obviously, you'll want to use your discretion regarding how much access you grant to new members of your team. Review the chart above to see how permissions are allocated. You'll notice they are organized to safeguard your content, only granting users access to the information needed to complete their respective roles or responsibilities.

Taxes and Banking

You know the motto: "Apps are a business."

As such, if you plan on collecting any forms of payment from your app, you'll not only need to complete tax forms but also add your bank information and sign off on a series of agreements.

To get your financial affairs in order simply log in to App Store Connect and click on "Agreements, Tax and Banking" *on the dashboard. Under the various tabs, you will execute specific tasks:*

Under the Agreements Tab

In this tab, complete both the Free and Paid app agreements. These agreements stipulate the conditions surrounding distributing and receiving payments for free or paid apps.

For future reference, if you ever end up transferring an app from one Apple account to another, you will also find notice of your app transfers in this section.

Under the Banking Tab

Set up and then add a bank account. Follow the directions and prompts to save your account info.

You don't necessarily have to add a business bank account to your Apple account. Personal accounts may be used; however, you can only have one bank account associated with your membership regardless of how many apps you manage on that profile, *so please choose wisely.*

Under the Tax Tab

If you're in the United States, complete your mandatory U.S. tax form as well as any other country tax forms necessary for running your app and then submit the required information.

Once you've handled your finance-related housekeeping for your app, there are some other prerequisites you'll want to familiarize yourself with.

Legal

To participate in the Apple Developer Program you'll need to agree to adhere to the *Apple Developer Program License Agreement*, which outlines the parameters around how you can use their products, platforms, and tools, in addition to providing rules around designing and developing your apps.[2]

You'll also want to look over Apple's *Review Guidelines*, where in section 5 you'll find a code of conduct and insights on navigating legal prerequisites like the following:

- Privacy
- Data collection, storage and sharing
- Health and health research
- Underage minors
- Location services
- Intellectual property
- Gambling and gaming

Many of these legal guidelines are imposed by law and, given the nature of politics, are subject to change at any time. They may also vary by country, as each has different laws for business operations.

Review Guidelines

Apple strives to provide a safe and secure premium experience for its end users. They do so in part by imposing high standards for app submissions and a rigorous review process each time you submit a new build or an update to the store.

The App Store reviewers assess each and every app submitted to the store in accordance with their compliance with the *App*

Store Review Guidelines,[3] Apple's detailed submission policies that span across five key categories: safety, performance, business, design, and legal. Millions of apps are submitted for review annually, but some are rejected before they can be admitted to the store. What follows are some common reasons why.

CRASHES AND BUGS

App Store Review Guideline 2.1—App Completeness

We will reject incomplete app bundles and binaries that crash or exhibit obvious technical problems.

Apple wants its users to feel confident they can download an app without the app crashing or causing potential damage to a user's phone. If your app has explicit bugs, broken links, loads slowly, or is regularly crashing, you need to take the time to stabilize your app before resubmitting. Your app needs to run fluidly and consistently before you can get approved.

INACCURATE SCREENSHOTS

App Store Review Guideline 2.3.—3 Performance: Accurate Metadata

Screenshots should show the app in use, and not merely the title art, login page, or splash screen. They may also include text and image overlays (e.g., to demonstrate input mechanisms, such as an animated touch point or Apple Pencil) and show extended functionality on devices, such as the Touch Bar.[4]

While it's tempting to spruce up your app store screenshots with souped-up designs, remember that these images are intended to accurately depict your app's value and functionality. It's fine to show a little creativity, but app store screenshots must depict replicas of the app itself.

PRIVACY AND DATA COLLECTION

App Review Guideline 5.1.1—Legal—Privacy—Data Collection and Storage

All apps must include a link to their privacy policy in the App Store Connect metadata field and within the app in an easily accessible manner.[5]

All apps that appear in the iOS App Store are required to have a *privacy policy statement.* The policy must appear in your metadata as well as in your app. Most people opt to put the statement on the sign-in/sign-up page or landing page. Additionally, if your app is intended for children or has a subscription service in the app, a link must be provided to a Privacy Policy page outside of the app.

As a reminder, that privacy policy is expected to include address the following items:

- *Data retention policies: Apps are required by law to give a detailed explanation of what data they are collecting and how it is being used.*
- *Ability to withdraw consent: Users must be given an outlet to withdraw their consent to the company collecting their data.*
- *Contact info: Apps are required to have a direct link for support as well as contact information for app management.*

REPLICAS AND COPYCATS

App Store Review Guideline 4.1—Design: Copycats

Don't simply copy the latest popular app on the App Store, or make some minor changes to another app's name or UI and pass it off as your own.[6]

As I stated before, I'm a huge fan of clone apps to shorten your development time, but remember these code scripts are intended to replicate key components of existing apps, not rip them off completely. Without building new elements on top of the clone and customizing with original designs, it's just outright plagiarism.

While it's nearly impossible to commit all of Apple's guidelines to memory, there are a few best practices to increase your chances of getting approved the first time around:

- *Test your app for bugs and crashes:* If your reviewer is experiencing crashes, so will your users. Work these bugs out before submitting your build.
- *Submit complete and accurate app information:* Your metadata (the images, information, and text displayed on your app page) needs to be forthcoming and an accurate depiction of the app you're submitting.
- *Provide contact information and demo accounts:* If available, provide demo or login information to grant your reviewer easy access to the app, as well as up-to-date contact details in the event they need to reach you.
- *Enable back end services:* During app testing, many backend services are temporarily disabled. As you transition to a live environment, be sure your developer turns on these services, so your app store reviewer does not mistake them for an error.
- *Add app review notes:* When submitting your app, you can include detailed explanations to help your reviewers better understand non-obvious features and functionality.
- *Build and design for iOS:* I know this seems like a no-brainer, but it's not always so obvious when you're in the thick of things. When submitting your app and its corresponding screenshots, make such there are no mentions or depictions of Android devices or any other platforms. If reviewers can't

see that this app was built specifically for iOS, you may have a hard time getting it approved.

If you follow all these steps and your app still gets rejected, do not fret. Rejection on the App Store is simply redirection. I've been rejected more times than I can count, and each time, the App Store review team has provided detailed notes on the error or asked for clarity on the exact point of confusion so I could self-correct and promptly resubmit for approval.

Uploading Your iOS App

Uploading an app to the App Store may seem complicated, but it's not nearly as scary as people make it out to be. If you're non-technical, your development team will likely manage this process for you. However, as an entrepreneur, it's important to gain confidence in submitting your app independently in case your tech team isn't available.

The following steps will outline step-by-step how to submit your project to the store. Note that Apple is at liberty to modify this process at any given time, so it is subject to change. Additionally, the steps I will provide will be given under the assumption that your developer or development team has registered a *bundle ID* for your app. A bundle ID is a unique identifier that enables you to register, modify, or delete an app. It confirms that the app itself is bug-free and submission-ready and that you have an active Apple Developer Program account. To submit, you'll need

- a computer that runs Mac OS X and
- Xcode installed. Xcode is Apple's development environment for macOS. Developers use it to develop software for macOS, iOS, iPadOS, watchOS, and tvOS.

STEP 1: CREATE AN APP STORE CONNECT RECORD

Before you can release an app to the App Store, you have to create a record for it in App Store Connect. The record stores all the information needed to manage the app in the distribution process and for it to appear in the store. To generate a record:

1. Log in to App Store Connect and select the My Apps icon.
2. Click the + in the left-hand corner and choose New App from the drop-down.

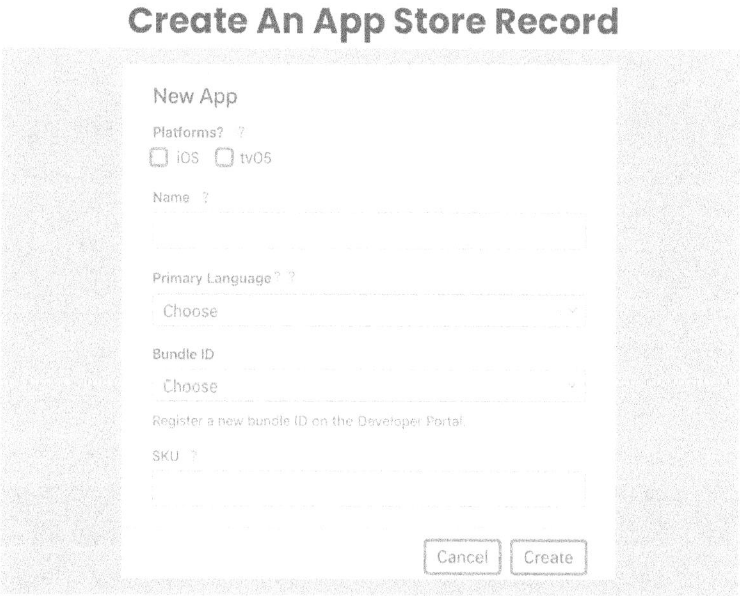

Create An App Store Record

You'll be prompted with a pop-up that requires assorted details surrounding your app. Some of these details are permanent, while others can be changed later; either way, be mindful about what you enter. Here are the fields you can anticipate:

- *Platforms:* Select the Apple platforms your app supports. Was your app intended just for the App Store, or was it was created specifically for Apple TV?

- *Name:* List the name you want users to see in the App Store. Remember, you have thirty characters in this section. Other than your name itself, feel free to include a few descriptive keywords to optimize user discovery. For example, "CultureCrush—Black Dating"
- *Primary language:* Identify the primary language the app's content will be displayed in. You can add localized translations for other languages later. If there is no translation provided for a particular language, the app will default to the app's primary language in countries in which that language is represented.
- *Bundle ID:* As a reminder, your developers should have registered a unique app identifier for your app in your Developer Account. The standard naming convention for a bundle ID is com.yourcompanyname.yourappname. No two apps can have the same ID. The ID selected must be the same one used during the *app archiving* (the bundling of the app in a format that can be submitted to the App Store).
- *Stock-keeping unit (SKU): A stock-keeping unit* is an optional value that allows you to tie app sales to internal SKU numbers in your accounting system. The field can include letters, numbers, hyphens, periods, or underscores but must begin with a letter or number. SKUs are particularly helpful to individuals or organizations managing more than one app on a single developer account. SKUs are not visible to your app users.
- *User access:* Select the members of your organization who can access the app.

Once you have completed this information, you will select the Create Account option listed and begin the process of archiving your app.

STEP 2: ARCHIVE YOUR APP AND UPLOAD TO THE APP STORE

Regardless of how you'd like to distribute the app, you must upload and archive it in *Xcode*, Apple's integrated development environment for building, storing, and debugging apps.

1. Open Xcode and select Generic iOS Device.
2. Choose Product from the top menu and click on Archive.
3. Your Xcode Organizer will be displayed, along with any existing archives. Select your current app build and click on Upload to App Store in the right-hand panel.
4. Select your credentials and click Choose. A window will appear in which you will need to select the Upload button in the bottom corner.

Once the upload is completed, you will see a success message. Please click the Done button and move to the next step.

Archive in Xcode

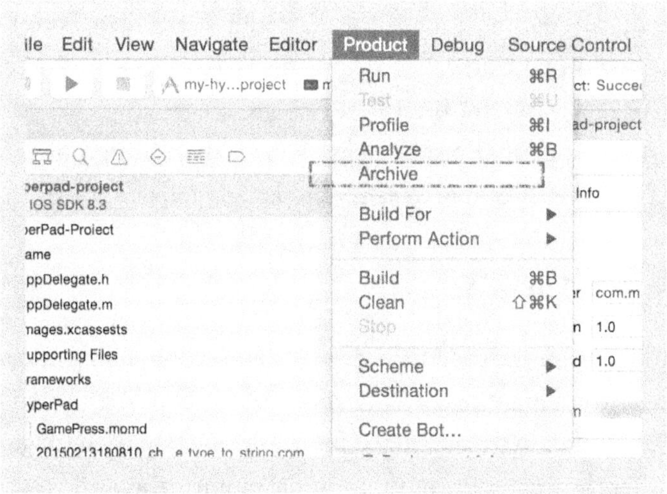

STEP 3: CREATE YOUR PRODUCT PAGE

Moving back over to App Store Connect, you'll find your app in the left-hand panel of the App Store tab. It will be marked with a yellow dot under the status level *Prepare for Submission.*

Prepare for Submission Status

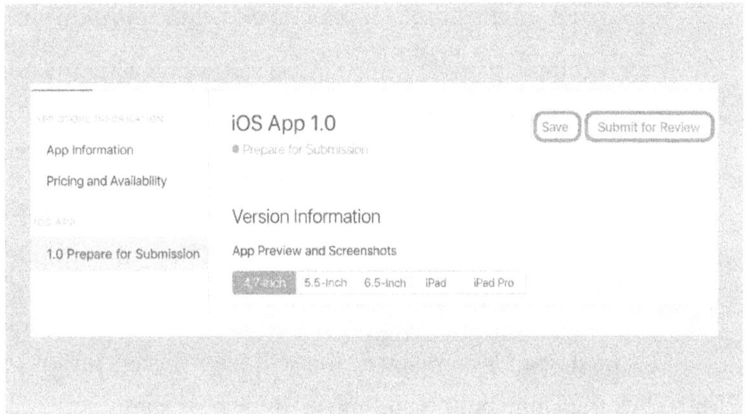

Remember the metadata and accompanying assets we built for the App Store in chapter 11? Well, it's their time to shine! Since we already covered these items I won't go into deep detail, but I will walk you through how they are organized and give a brief description of each as a refresher.

Your App Store product page will be divided into three distinct sections: *iOS App, General,* and *In-App Purchases.*

Section 1: iOS App

The first leg of the product page is focused on providing information surrounding the current version of the app. Even when you make updates to the app in the future, this section of the page will be where you enter the most up-to-date information:

- *App previews*
- *App screenshots*
- *App icon*
- *Promotional text*
- *Description*
- *Keywords*
- *Support URL*
- *Marketing URL*
- *App clip:* A relatively new feature from Apple, this section allows users to access a small part of the app through a Safari browser without actually installing the app.
- *Version number:* This is the version of the app you will be submitting; it should match the one in Xcode. As you make more updates to an app, the version number will steadily increase (e.g., Version 1.0 , Version 1.1, Version 1.2).
- *Age rating:* Primarily created to protect children and inform parents, this rating is assigned by Apple to safeguard more vulnerable populations from particular types of content such as violence or nudity. Apps are rated by the frequency and intensity of these types of content.
- *Copyright:* Displays the owner of the rights to the app, for example: Copyright (c) 2022, TipOff Games, LLC.
- *Routing app coverage file:* This file manages the geographic coverage files in apps that use location to provide routing information.
- *The build:* Your archived app, ready for submission to the store.

Upload the app build you'd like to submit by clicking the blue Select a Build button. A dialog box will display all available builds. Upon selecting the build of your choice, you may be asked questions about whether your app uses encryption; respond accordingly. Afterward, you will see additional options for the selected build, including how your app should be released. You have the option of releasing your app:

- *Manually:* Once you're notified that the app was approved by reviewers, you click a Release button to make it publicly available.
- *Automatically:* Once the app is approved, it will automatically appear in the store within twenty-four hours.
- *Automatically with date restriction:* Upon approval of the app, the app will be released on a specified date selected by you.

Your app will be reviewed by one of Apple's reviewers from around the world. With literally thousands of submissions pouring in daily, you want to make it as easy as possible for them to complete your review without incident.

In the App Review Notes section, provide your reviewer with these items:

- Demo account login and password
- Your contact information, in the event the reviewer needs to contact you
- Detailed notes about non-obvious features of functionality—things they wouldn't know or be able to assume by looking at the app at first glance

Section 2: General

This portion of the page holds standard and operational app listing information such as the following:

- *Subtitle*
- *App categories*
- *Pricing availability:* Not to be confused with in-app purchases, pricing details how much a user has to pay, if anything, to download an app. Prices for apps may be specified for a specific period of time; however, you cannot convert a free app into a paid app. If you wanted to replace your free app with a paid app, you would need to republish the paid app with a different app ID. Then you could deprecate the older, free version or simply keep both the free and paid versions available in the store.
- *Availability:* This function allows you to govern the countries or regions where the app will be available.
- *App privacy:* Again, Apple requires that all apps submit a privacy policy for consideration for the store. More recently, they have added a Data Types section, which outlines to users what specific types of data your app collects. As an app owner, you must clarify how the data you collect is used and if that data is linked to your user's identity or for tracking purposes.
- *Ratings and reviews:* Your ratings can heavily impact user acquisition and how users view your app. When new ratings and reviews come in, view and respond to them here. Use this as an opportunity to connect with users and address their questions and concerns.

- *Version history:* See the full history of your app build uploads and their current statuses in the App Store.

Section 3: In-App Purchases

Remember, if your app contains virtual goods or services that users will pay for, you have in-app purchases. In-app purchases are divided into four different categories, but you are always free to offer multiple types of purchases in the same app simultaneously.

- *Consumable:* Consumables are virtual goods that can be depleted as they're used and can be repurchased again. They tend to be popular in gaming apps.
- *Non-consumable:* Premium upgrades or features that are purchased once and don't expire are non-consumable.
- *Auto-renewable subscription:* Automatic recurring subscription payments provide ongoing access to content, services, or premium features.
- *Non-renewing subscription:* Access to services or content for a fixed or limited time ends on the stated date.

In-app purchases can be configured by adding each purchase type's title, description, price, and availability in App Store Connect.

After inputting your information across all three sections, go to the upper right-hand corner of the page and press *Save.*

Step 4: Submit Your App for Review

Your metadata is ready. Your build is bug-free. You are ready to submit for review.

Click the Submit for Review button to move the build forward.

Immediately after submitting, you'll be asked to complete three questionnaires:

3 questionnaires

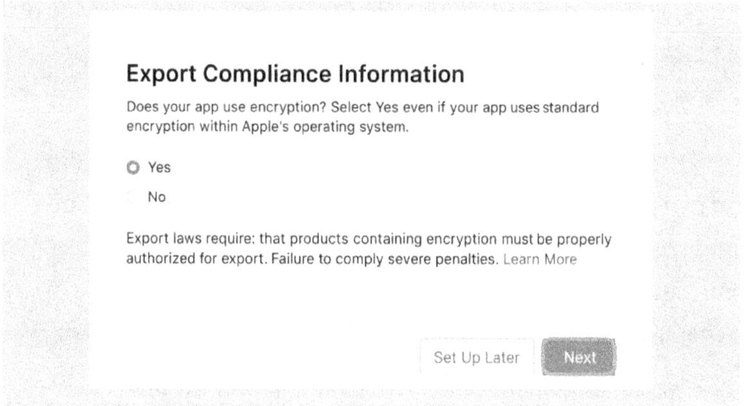

1. *Export compliance:* Since Apple's servers are in the United States, any submissions to the App Store that are distributed outside of the United States are subject to export laws, regardless of where you are submitting from. If your app uses or accesses encryption, this is considered an export of encryption software, making you subject to both U.S. encryption export requirements and import requirements to the countries you distribute to.
2. *Content rights:* Apps that contain content from third-party sources must demonstrate that they have the necessary rights to display it.
3. *Advertising identifiers:* Each Apple device has an assigned device identifier that advertisers use to track data so they can deliver customized advertising—without revealing the user's personal information. As an app entrepreneur, if you

are using Apple's identifiers you must reveal how and in what capacity you'll be using them.

After completing the questionnaires, click Submit. Your app status is now *Waiting for Review.*

Celebrate yourself, YOU DID IT! You're about to cross the finish line.

"How long will I be in review?"

The review process could take anywhere from a few days to a few weeks. It is different for each app. Apple states that around 50 percent of apps are reviewed in twenty-four hours, and over 90 percent are reviewed in forty-eight hours.[7] I find this to be pretty accurate, although your nerves can make it feel much longer.

"Once I submit, how do I check the status of my app?"

You can check the status of your app at any given time in App Store Connect. Visit the left-side menu, and under the General section, select the Version History subcategory.

After you submit your app for review, you will also receive email notifications at each stage of the submission process.

"What if I get rejected?"

Don't fret! You're not alone; tons of apps get rejected annually. To get back in the game, you simply need to make the necessary corrections and resubmit your app for review. Start by visiting your Resolution Center in App Store Connect to see detailed notes from your reviewer, who will outline the exact error and what needs to be done for your app to be compliant.

If you believe the app was wrongly or unfairly rejected, you can submit clarifying notes back to the reviewer or escalate the issue by submitting an appeal.

"I was approved! When will I see my app in the store?"

Congratulations!

Once your app is approved, you will be notified by email, and your status will be updated to *Ready for Sale*. If you selected automatic release, your app is likely to be visible in the App Store within twenty-four hours. If you selected manual release for your release type, you will need to click the Release button to add it to the store.

"What do I do now?"

Continue to monitor and manage your app from your App Store Connect dashboard. You'll get up-to-date critical usage and download analytics, in addition to being able to track your sales, ratings, and reviews.

Submitting Your App to Google Play

And now we're off to Google Play! With nearly 4,000 apps currently released daily, Google Play is the undisputed leader in the distribution of Android apps, and having your app there creates an excellent opportunity to gain global exposure. Keep reading as I outline the step-by-step process of submitting your app to this market.

Accounts and Assigning Roles

If you haven't done so already, set up your Google Developer account. This requires you to have a Google account.

Use a new or existing Google account to sign in, read, and agree to the Google Play Developer distribution agreement and Google Play Console Terms of Service, and then pay a onetime registration fee, which is $25 at the time of this writing.

After paying the fee, you'll be prompted to set up your developer profile, including your developer name, email address, website (if applicable), and phone number. Note: Your developer name will be visible to users on the Play Store, so choose wisely.

Once you've completed your registration, you might wait up to forty-eight hours for your application to be approved.

Taxes and Banking

Once approved, if you plan to publish a paid app or have in-app purchases, you will need to link your now-approved Developer account with a Google Merchant account.

To do this:

1. Sign in to your Google Play account console and click Reports.
2. You'll see an option to select Financial Reports, which will lead you to "Set up a merchant account."
3. Fill out your details and submit to automatically link your console. In the future, you will not only be able to manage and examine your app sales from this page but also review your monthly payouts.

Legal

All apps on Google Play must adhere to the Google Play Developer Program policies and satisfy legal requirements to be listed and stay in the store.

The platform requires each app to have a Privacy Policy page to detail how you will treat user and device data. I would also strongly recommend adding terms of use or terms and conditions, as well as an *end-user license agreement,* or EULA,[8] which is an agreement between you and your users that outlines how they can and cannot use the app, licensing fees, and use of intellectual property.

These documents will be housed on your app's Content page, where you'll be able to update and manage the information and keep the Play Store assured that your app is safe for its intended users.

Review Guidelines

A big misconception in the development world is that Google Play's review process is less strenuous than the App Store. The reality is that despite having over three million apps in their marketplace, Google is rumored to reject nearly 55 percent[9] of submitted apps.

Many of these rejected apps were likely in violation of the Google Developer Policies[10]. Google's Developer Distribution Agreement not only details how apps need to be developed, but how they should be updated and supported to continually meet the store's standard of quality. Some of the most common reasons the Play Store rejects app submissions include:

Intellectual Property[11]

Developer Distribution Agreement 11.1—Representations and Warranties

You represent and warrant that You have all Intellectual Property Rights in and to Your Product(s), including the right to monetize Your Product(s) on Your own behalf and not solely acting as an agent or appointee on behalf of any other person.

With the volume of apps being submitted daily, there are bound to be some copyright issues on the platform. However, Google Play takes a proactive approach to monitoring intellectual property by setting strict policies and providing best practices to help you steer clear of infringement.

As a founder, you'll want to browse the store to study any prospective competitors. Review their titles, visual design, logos and branding, metadata, and even in-app elements to ensure your app is not a poor copy of an existing product. Strive for originality in the design, code, and content.

Inappropriate Content

Developer Content Policy—Content

Before submitting an app, ask yourself if your app is appropriate for Google Play and compliant with local laws.

Your app's content will be reviewed. Apps that contain violence or racist, sexual, or inflammatory imagery will be rejected. Google Play provides a very transparent shortlist with detailed explanations of materials that should be clearly identified and are subject to rejection or potential rejection if not structured properly. These categories include the following:

- Content involving child endangerment
- Sexual or profane content
- Misleading financial products and services
- Gambling and contests
- Illegal activities
- User-generated content
- Health-related content, including prescription drugs and unapproved substances
- Blockchain-based services

Improper App Rating

Developer Content Policy—Store Listing and Promotion

The promotion and visibility of your app dramatically affects store quality. Avoid spammy store listings, low-quality promotion, and efforts to artificially boost app visibility on Google Play.

Prior to publishing your app, Google Play requires that you select an app rating. This rating system is provided to Google in affiliation with the International Age Rating Coalition (IARC)[12] to help forewarn users of content that may potentially be sensitive or inappropriate, in particular to children.

To ensure apps are classified appropriately, each app submitter must complete a questionnaire that will help to identify the right age category the app is appropriate for. You should strive to submit accurate and relevant information so that you are properly graded for your intended audience. Those who try to deceive the moderation team to be underrated could risk permanent rejection from the store.

Uploading Your Android App

Let me congratulate you again for making it this far. You've powered through the ideation process, rounds of design, development, and endless testing to be here, and you're only clicks away from Android deployment. As you prepare to publish your app in Google Play, you'll need to cross your t's and dot your i's by checking the following ahead of submission:

- *App size and format:* Google Play accepts only two release formats for apps: Android app bundle (AAB) and Android package (APK). You know how PNG and JPG are file formats for pictures? This is kind of along the same lines but for apps. These app formats are actually similar in nature, as AABs were created in response to a need for a larger, more efficient file format to APK. To date, the size limit for Android versions 2.3 and higher is 100 MB. So if your app's file size exceeds this, you and your developer will need to either need to use an APK expansion file, which Google will host and store for free, or use an AAB, which allows for up to a 150 MB compressed download size.13

- *Unique bundle ID:* To uniquely identify each application in an ecosystem, each app is given a package name, or unique bundle ID, in the app's manifest file. This ID will be tied to the package over the life of this app and cannot be changed after distribution.
- *Signed app release:* All apps must be digitally signed with a developer signing certificate. The certificate can only be generated once.

STEP 1: CREATE YOUR APPLICATION

Log in to the Developer Console and locate the All Applications tab on the main menu. A Create Application button will appear, and once selected, you'll be routed to a store entry page and prompted to provide information as follows:

- *Your app's default language*
- *Your app's name:* Your app's name can be changed in the future.
- *Whether your app is a free app or a paid app:* Selecting the free app option is a permanent decision, as free apps cannot be converted to paid apps on Google Play. However, if you

select the paid app option, you can change the app's price at your convenience. I'll share more about this a little later in the chapter.

- *A user-support email address*

Create Application (Android)

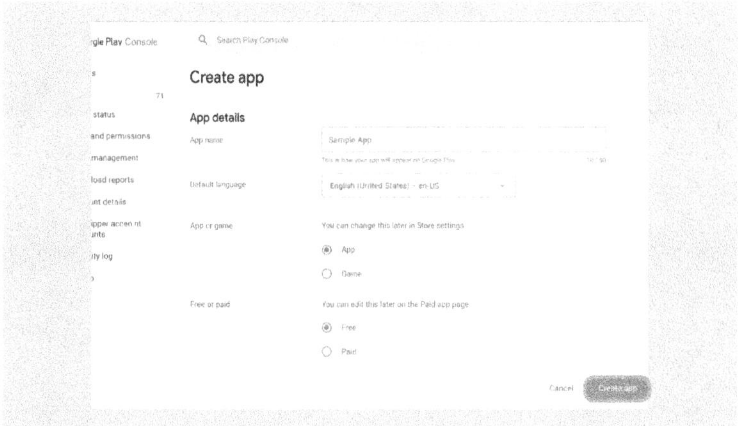

Once completed, you'll need to acknowledge the required policies and laws in the *Declarations section and accept the signing terms of service before clicking Create.*

STEP 2: YOUR GOOGLE PLAY LISTING

Capturing the attention of potential users often starts with a compelling app store listing. This page will contain the most important information about your app to entice users with all the relevant details before downloading. It also provides an opportunity to boost your visibility in the store with relevant keywords for app store optimization.

Your Google Play App Page

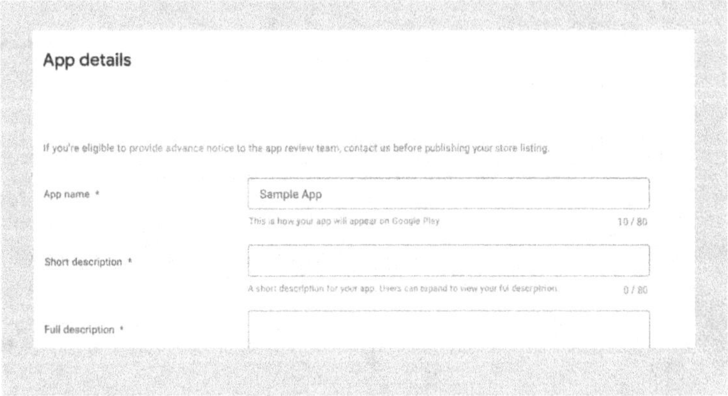

You'll be asked to provide the following:

- *A product description*
- *Screenshots*
- *An icon*
- *Feature graphic*
- *Promo video*
- *Tags:* related keywords that help users search and find your app
- *Localization*
- *App type*
- *App categories*
- *Contact details*
- *A privacy policy*

If you need to take a break while completing this page, you can click Save Draft anytime and come back later.

STEP 3: UPLOADING YOUR APK OR ABB

When you're ready, head over to the main menu again and select App Releases.

App Releases Button

You'll immediately be asked to select the type of release you'd like to deploy and be given four options:

1. Internal test
2. Closed test
3. Open test
4. Production release

You may recall from chapter 12 that the first three options—internal, closed, and open—are forms of alpha and beta testing. With these options, Google Play is providing you with an environment to test and improve your app before its release. The production release option, however, is reserved for the live version of your finalized app. This is the option you will select when wanting to publish the app publicly. Once you make your choice, you'll be directed to the next page where you can select Create Release to go to the production page. From here you will do the following:

1. *Make an app signing selection:* All APKs must be digitally signed with a certificate before being installed or updated. You have the option of using Google Play's app signing feature or opting out to sign in locally.
2. *Select* Browse Files *to look up your file.*
3. *Choose the correct APK or AAB files to upload:* Complete the on-screen instructions to name your release and provide release notes. This written documentation accompanies new or recently updated software launches.
4. *Select* Review *to confirm your app release.*
5. *Click* Save *upon completion.*

STEP 4: CONTENT RATING

One of the most critical steps in the app submission process is rating your app. As we discussed earlier in the chapter, all apps on Google Play must be assigned a rating to be active in the market. These ratings are assigned based on your responses to a questionnaire.

App Rating Selection

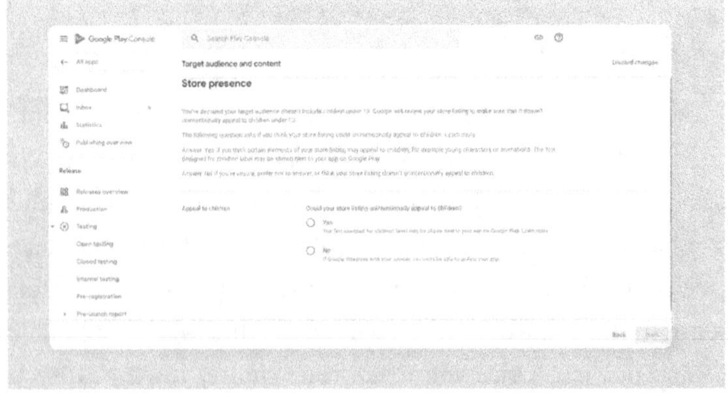

If an app is listed as "Unrated," the app could be removed from the store, and any misrepresentations of your app's content could lead to a permanent ban.

To start your survey, select Store Presence from the main menu, click on Content Rating, and complete the following steps:

1. Select Continue.
2. Enter and confirm your email address.
3. Select your app category from the available options.
4. Accurately and truthfully respond to the survey.
5. Click Save Questionnaire.
6. Select Calculate Rating to see your app's rating on the Google Play Store.
7. Confirm your app's rating by clicking Apply Rating.

STEP 5: PRICING AND DISTRIBUTION

You're in the apps business now. You'll want to approach this portion of the upload process with a plan that combines strategic pricing and regional targeting to achieve product-market fit. Fortunately, Google offers a helping hand by way of its flexible features.

The platform allows you to set your pricing and change it whenever you feel inclined. It also gives you the freedom to control your distribution or pick the countries where your app will be available. These settings present an opportunity for you to streamline your growth in a calculated and intentional way.

Before we get into your pricing instructions, here's one last reminder: On Google Play, you can change a paid app to a free one, but you cannot convert a free app to a paid one. If you find yourself needing to convert a free app to a paid one, you will have to create a new paid app and then disable the original free version.

Pricing Left Menu

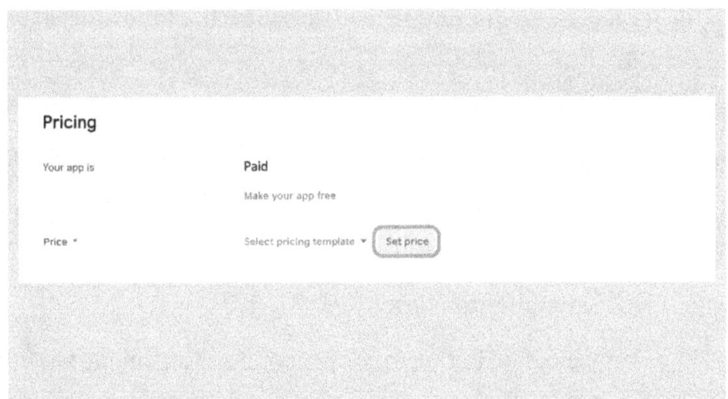

To set your pricing and distribution plan in motion, navigate to the Pricing and Distribution option on the left menu and follow these steps:

1. Select whether your app will be free or paid.
2. Determine which countries your app will be released in.
3. If your app is suitable for children, select Yes; if otherwise, select No.
4. If your app contains ads, check Yes; if not, check No.

STEP 6: PUBLISH YOUR APP

You're closing in on the finish line and inching closer to seeing that app of yours on Google Play.

To round out this step and start submitting and publishing your app, you'll need to go back to the App Releases *tab on the main menu.*

Pricing Left Menu

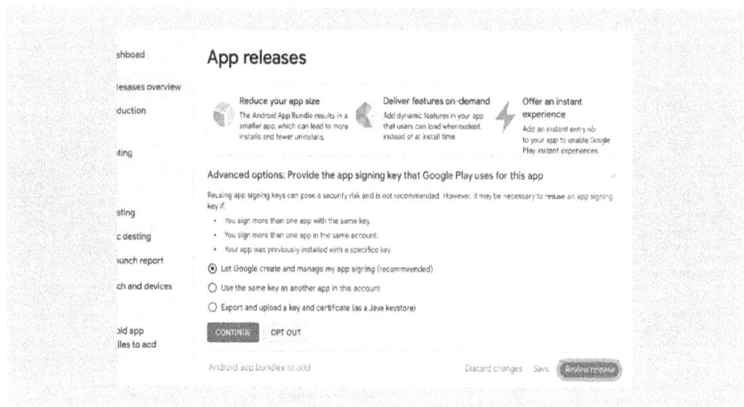

From there, you'll do the following:

1. Select Manage Production.
2. Click Edit Release.
3. Go to the bottom right portion of the page to select the Review button.
4. Select the Start rollout to production option.
5. Wrap up the process by clicking Confirm when prompted.

And then we wait . . .

But don't fret, you'll have your outcome soon! Apps often go through Google Play's review process within a matter of hours. At the most, you'll only be waiting a few days. You can check your app status on your app console anytime.

Bravo! Congrats on crossing yet another major milestone, appreneur.

Chapter checklist

For iOS:

- [ ] Assign user roles (if necessary).
- [ ] Complete tax and bank information.
- [ ] Complete the free and paid app agreements.
- [ ] Sync the bank account of your choice.
- [ ] Familiarize yourself with the App Store Review Guidelines.
- [ ] Create an App Store Connect record.
- [ ] Archive app and upload it to the App Store.
- [ ] Create a product page. 9. Submit your app for review.

For Android:

- [ ] Check app size.
- [ ] Check file format.
- [ ] Assign bundle ID.
- [ ] If applicable, set up Google Merchant Account.
- [ ] Review Google Play Developer Program policies.
- [ ] Draft your EULA.
- [ ] Complete rating questionnaire.
- [ ] Complete store listing.
- [ ] Submit app.

CHAPTER 14

Engaging and Attracting Users

Hold up, wait a minute. Y'all thought we were finished?

Stepping into appreneur life means you've got a business baby to grow, and the work is ongoing. You've cleared a massive hurdle by actually getting your app into the stores. But if we're keeping it 100, you've got to know that just because you've built it doesn't mean they will come.

This chapter will provide a high-level overview of the key considerations for marketing your app to attract users and then retain them once they've downloaded.

Marketing Best Practices

With millions of apps available in each app store, it's too easy for potential users to get lost in a sea of competitors and distractions. While there is no surefire way to secure a download or convert customers, there are some common industry practices and tactics that have been effective for other founders.

As you start to piece together your *user acquisition strategy*—your marketing plan to attract new users and persuade them to purchase—pick practices you believe will work best for your business, budget, and audience and then test what works best for you. What follows are some suggestions, in no particular order, to keep top of mind as you begin to strategize.

Add Value Outside of the App

Selling your services to a customer is both an inside and an outside job. While your content and other supporting assets are what will likely drive users to download, it's what's inside the app that will keep them there.

To create engaging external content, revisit your persona's initial problem. What are some of the customer's underlying emotions that are tied to their issue? Perhaps solving the problem would make them feel, deep down, more empowered or informed, or make them feel seen and heard. Next, think about the mediums and outlets your audience frequents and then start using those channels to provide complimentary content that directly addresses those emotions. Perhaps you could create a blog where you share relevant thought leadership on your industry or a private Facebook group where users can share their opinions on both your app and its industry.

Do Things That Don't Scale

User acquisition, as a practice, is typically thought of as a game of optimization: "How do I quickly secure the largest audience for the least amount of money?" But when you're still at an early stage, many of the most impactful things you can do to yield big results are tedious, time-intensive, and may cost quite a bit.

Dating app Tinder acquired its first fifteen thousand users by traveling from college to college, where their then-CMO would present the app to chapters of her sorority and encourage members to sign up. She would then introduce the app to their corresponding brother fraternity, whose members were excited to meet new girls on campus. Tinder would also occasionally host themed parties that required app download for entry, a strategy we borrowed when marketing CultureCrush in Washington, DC. Obviously, quite a bit of planning, time, and money went into executing Tinder's first tour, but with Tinder ultimately becoming a leading dating app within a matter of months, I would say it was well worth it.[1]

INVESTOR INSIGHT

"I think sometimes founders try to focus too much on building a scalable product before building a product that solves a problem or a product that their customers want to use, which is really, really important.

When building your product, you may have to do things that don't scale. In the beginning, give your customers white-glove service. Make sure that you're actually there, hand-holding them, walking them through the process so that you can learn along with them.

Your product should be built in a way that when you want to transition from doing things that don't scale to get you off the ground, that it has the infrastructure to quickly turn around to doing things that are far more scalable."

~McKeever "Mac" Conwell II, Founder and Managing Partner of RareBreed Ventures[2]

Create Viral Loops

A *viral loop*[3] is a system or mechanism that entices users of your app to refer the product to others. It works as a loop because each new user ideally follows the process of inviting a new group of users, who will in turn do the same, enabling your user base to market the app on your behalf. Viral loops are often tied to incentives like account upgrades, early access, or complementary tokens, but in a perfect world, the user would find the product or service so valuable that they feel compelled to tell people about it, as the app is organically structured to be shared with others.

One of the best examples of viral loops gone right was conducted by Robinhood, the stock trading and investing app. Ahead of their launch, they incentivized eager early adopters to spread the word about the app through a gamified waitlist program. As people referred their friends to the app, they moved higher up the waitlist, effectively capitalizing on their competitive nature and desire for early access. This strategy led to rapid growth and a substantial user base of over one million people upon launch.[4]

A/B Testing

You could have a great app, but the wrong language or imagery could turn the right users off. I know you've invested a lot of time into giving your app a certain look and feel, but try not to get too attached. As users begin to interact with your app, your key learnings from their usage will lead it to evolve from month to month or even day to day.

To make sure you're headed in the right direction I recommend *A/B testing*: experimenting with running tests with at least two variants of content, imagery, or even links to see what statistically converts or resonates better with your audience.[5]

Also known as split testing, this technique helps you minimize risk and create content efficiently to keep users engaged and visually pleased.

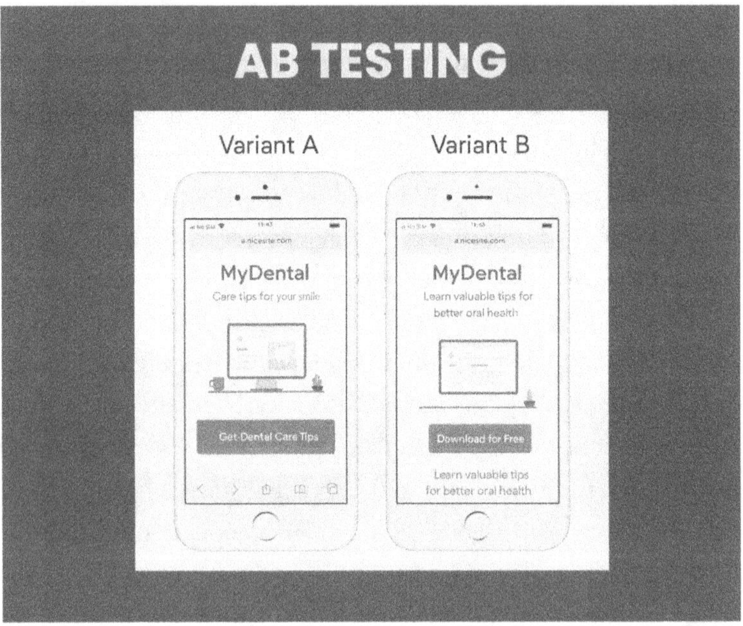

As you collect insights, test variations of imagery and content to see what performs better in regard to engagement and conversions. Did you get more clicks? Were more purchases made?

Encourage Reviews and Ratings

Apps are similar to restaurants in the sense that reviews and ratings are often the deciding factor before a person selects them. As well, your ratings and reviews directly impact your ranking in the app store's search results. Positive reviews and high ratings can help you increase your visibility, drive traffic to your listing, and build your brand reputation. Don't be afraid to ask for reviews both inside and outside of the app.

Negative reviews are inevitable, but you should take them in stride. Since both app stores allow you to respond to reviews, these interactions can be a great opportunity to connect with customers, educate them on the product, and gather feedback to identify areas for improvement.

Localize for the Markets You Serve

Lastly, consider localizing your app, or adapting the app, its content, and its app store listing to appeal to a geographically specific target market. This means converting the cultural, linguistic, and even technical requirements to the markets where demand may come from.

When my CultureCrush partner and I realized that many of our downloads were coming from Brazil, we quickly realized we needed to translate the app into Brazilian Portuguese. After all, how could they enjoy our app if they couldn't even read it?

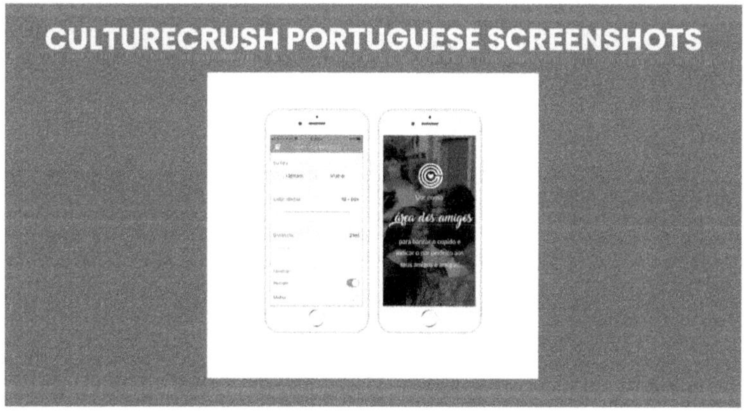

We eventually went as far as to modify our business model in that market to be more economically friendly and overhauled our app listing to make it culturally conscious.

While I wouldn't recommend immediately localizing for every country, as that could get costly, I do recommend making strategic predictions, then following the data on where you are getting the most traction and optimizing for that location. Localization doesn't necessarily guarantee downloads, but it does offer quite a bit of strategic support for your other user acquisition tactics.

Marketing Tactics

You can complement many of the strategic practices we discussed above with marketing tactics, or individual steps and actions to achieve your user acquisition goals. Keep reading to explore several proven methods for increasing downloads.

App Store Optimization (ASO)

Similar to ratings and reviews, keywords are crucial for amplifying your app's visibility in the market. App Store optimization (ASO) is the process of utilizing those keywords, tags, and other forms of content in your app listing to boost your app's visibility, which in turn helps to increase organic downloads.

ASO is important because most apps are found by direct search in the App Store. That means when a person searches for a new app in the App Store, they likely type the name of the app itself or some term associated with it. When this happens, you ideally want your app to be among the top search results. If you haven't optimized your page with keywords, your odds simply aren't as good.

Some freelancers and agencies specialize in ASO, but you can also subscribe to ASO and keyword search tools to find what people are searching for both domestically and in international markets.

Public Relations

As a former publicist myself (I've lived many lives), I could not leave public relations off the list. P*ublic relations (PR)* is the strategic communications process that influences public perception of a person, brand, or company and is often associated with securing media placements on their behalf.

A *Forbes* or *Black Enterprise* article can change the game for a promising new app, but with PR, timing is always key.

The best time to retain a publicist is when your product is stable, it has some initial traction, and you don't need immediate results. PR can often be a tactic that's slow to cook. A PR cycle can take weeks or even months to get you the placements you want to see, and with journalists receiving hundreds of pitches daily, it can be easy for your product to get overlooked.

As a founder, you also need to be mindful of the time it takes to dedicate to this tactic. Once you bring a publicist on board, they will likely line up a constant stream of interviews and contributing articles for you to participate in. Running an app is already a demanding job, and if you don't have the capacity to actively participate in these engagements, both you and your publicist could be wasting valuable time and resources.

Content Marketing

Earlier we discussed the strategy of adding value outside the app. *content marketing*, or the act of creating, publishing, and distributing content for a targeted audience, is the tactic that helps you deliver on that.[6]

From YouTube videos to e-books, you have a variety of mediums to choose from, but the most impactful content follows what I like to call the 3E Impact Strategy. This approach ensures your content aims to educate, entertain, and empower, all while striving to be intentional.

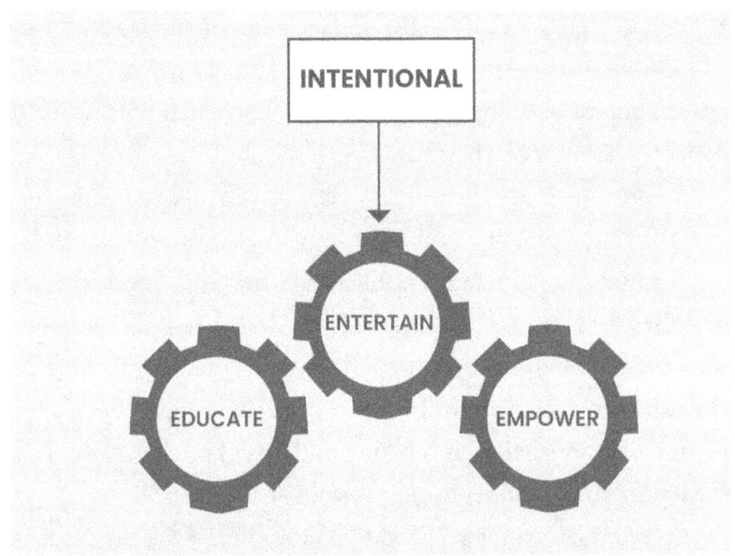

When I say intentional, I don't just mean when it comes to reaching your audience; the content must be published with the purpose of promoting your company. So while you're giving away the good stuff, remember to keep your app at the helm. That means setting a goal for each piece of content and integrating tools like email opt-ins and calls to action in each piece to ensure that you're driving not just conversation but also downloads.

Social Media

In this digital day and age, social media feels like a given for any business, but even it must be used with caution. Pursue the platforms your audience is most active on and strive to knock your content out of the park.

Being present on every medium sounds like a good idea, until you have to manage them all successfully. You know what's arguably worse than no page at all? A poorly managed one.

Even when you feel like you're crushing it, take the time to audit the social media accounts you do have and ask yourself these questions:

- What are my engagement and growth rates? What do they tell me about the effectiveness of my content?
- From the content on this page, both in the feed and in the bio, is it clear that I have an app?
- Am I clearly articulating the value and benefits of my app?
- Is it clear from this page how to access and download my app?

Before I launched my first app, Alchomy, I grew our Instagram page to over fifteen thousand users. Using the 3E Impact Strategy, my media mix was an interesting mashup of quotes and jokes, travel recaps, reviews, and "spirit stories" featuring many of our bartender followers telling interesting stories from behind the bar. The content led to buy-in and interest in the app while simultaneously fostering a feeling of community. When the app was finally ready for release, I was able to roll it out to an eager audience of followers and drive downloads by simply adding the link in my bio and including calls to action in my content.

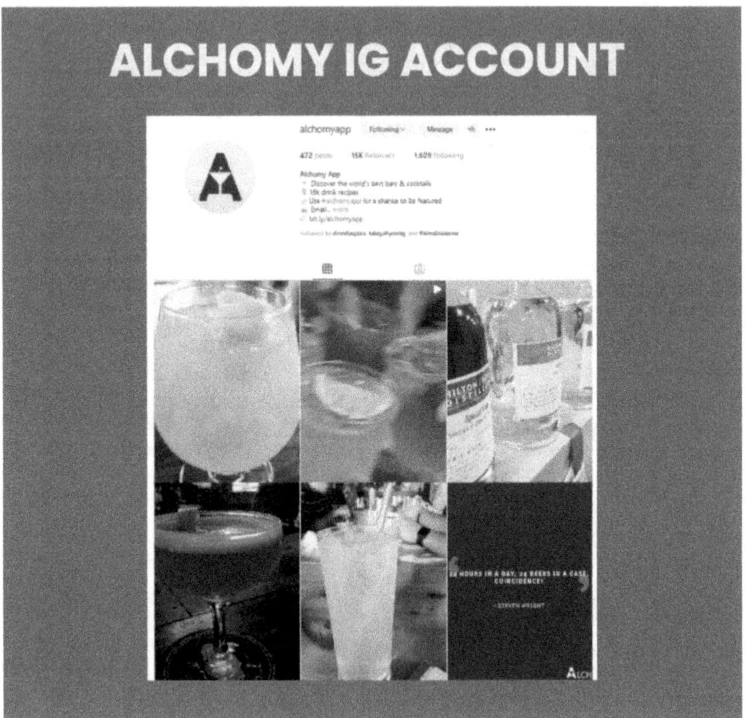

Paid Marketing

Paid marketing is simply advertising. Whether you're paying for premium placement in the app stores (yes, app store ads are a thing) or for your content to be amplified across a social media channel, you are spending money to have your product promoted to the targeted audience of your choice.

While paid ads do tend to convert better than organic content, that doesn't mean they are always effective. Monitoring and iteration are the name of the game here. As you run ads, you'll be provided with day-to-day campaign insights. Review these daily, as you don't want to keep paying for ads that aren't bringing the results you want. Conversion tracking metrics will show you what is working, what isn't, and what could be better optimized.

Influencer Marketing

Influencer marketing is a form of paid marketing where a person with an audience at their disposal is compensated to influence potential buyers of a product or service by recommending or promoting it to them, typically on social media.[7]

Be sure to inform the influencer of your goal for the campaign. Set parameters around the type of content you would like posted, when you would like it delivered, and any key points they should include in their messaging. Like ads, influencer marketing can be measured. Once you execute a campaign, be sure to review engagement rates, reach, conversions, and return on investment.

While you can't always predict how an influencer's audience will react to the promotion, there are a few tactics that have proven to be effective in increasing conversion:

- *Discount codes:* Personalized promo codes that offer a deal or discount
- *Deep linking:* Embedded links that are incorporated into the content, like swiping up or posting a link in an Instagram Story

If you're pre-product, you could also opt for a simple awareness campaign, where the influencer tells their audience about you and your product in order to drive sign-ups on a landing page or increase your page following.

For TipOff, our word guessing game, we sponsored a post with a comedian we enjoyed on Instagram. While she did not include the link to our game in her bio (as that option required an additional fee), the increased awareness from her followers led to a massive spike in downloads.

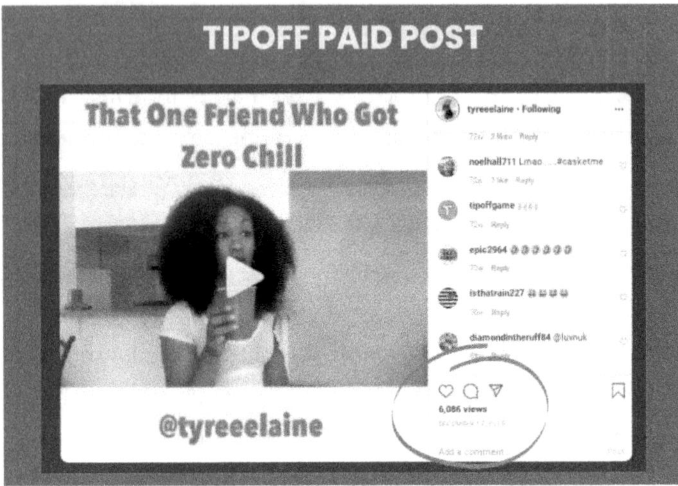

The post performed so well that she actually reposted it months later, and we got to experience a second wave of downloads. Influencer traffic often comes in waves; you'll experience a sharp increase in traffic, but because social media moves so quickly, that visibility often goes as fast as it comes.

Remember, getting your app into the stores is just the beginning; attracting and retaining users is where the real work begins. By developing a solid marketing plan, engaging your users, and continuously iterating based on feedback, you're well on your way to achieving long-term success with your new business.

CHAPTER 15

Maintaining Momentum: Retention and App Upkeep

You've heard me say that just because we build it doesn't mean they will come. But what's often left unsaid is that even if they do come, it doesn't guarantee they'll stay.

So in this section, we'll be talking about how to make your app "sticky," and the art of increasing user retention. *App user retention* is the ability of a product to retain a user over a period of time. Retention is defined many ways, depending on the type of product you're working on, but generally in the app world we say you've retained a user if they come back to the app one or more times during a thirty-day period.[1]

Now you're probably thinking, "Once in thirty days? That's pathetic! I know people will love my app and they'll come back at least a few times after they download." While I appreciate the confidence, understand that over 21 percent of new users, on average, abandon an app immediately after one use.[2] Your app could be absolutely amazing, and you should still anticipate losing nearly 20 percent of your audience. Now imagine your app is less than amazing—which is highly likely, since nobody gets it just right their first time around.

And this is why focusing on user retention is important. You've spent your time and money getting users here. Now, let's explore a few tactics that may keep them here. We'll start inside the app and work our way outside of it.

Optimizing Onboarding

Let's start with onboarding. Since this process is the first thing people will see when they enter your app, it is also where they are most likely to drop off.

When users enter your app, you should immediately emphasize your value proposition. This doesn't have to be a full explanation of what you do; it's just a small reminder of what problem the app will solve for them. This could be your tagline prominently featured or an animated gif of your app at work.

Next, highlight the core features. These are the need-to-know app elements users will be using most often. This might be a how-it-works slider or even an interactive walkthrough where you point to key features and share what they do. It helps if you have progress indicators, such as little dots at the bottom of the screen that display how many steps are included in this process.

Concisely show your new users how to use the app and the next steps they should take.

Depending on how your login process is set up, you might ask for information from your user at this point, but you'll want to keep this short and sweet. Think about how many times you've filled out an application only to realize that there are dozens of additional fields to complete. Ain't nobody got time for that! Remember to use contextual onboarding to collect only the information that's necessary to complete this step.

Another great way of collecting data without giving "information overload" vibes is with social media logins. By simply adding a sign-up with a third-party service like Facebook or LinkedIn, you can collect relevant user data while saving them time along the way.

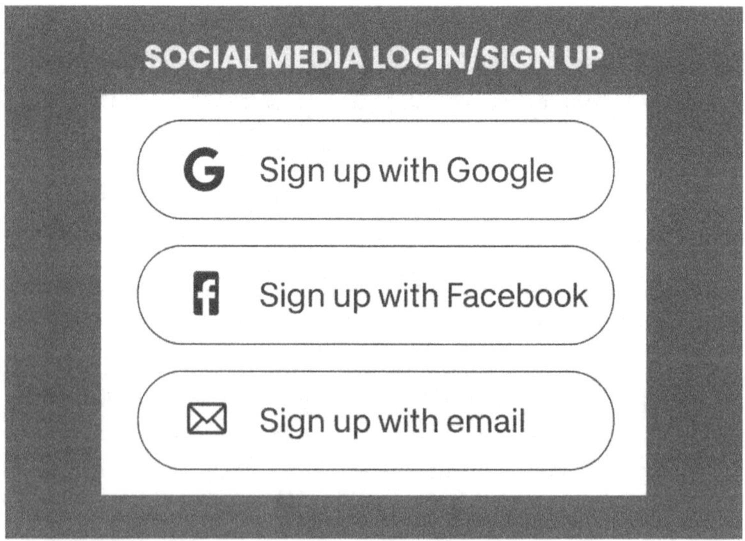

Make signing up or logging in easier with social media.

Always end your onboarding process with a call to action, like a button to get started or a prompt for them to take the next steps. People's attention span is so short these days. Even if they get through your entire onboarding process, the slightest of distractions could cause them to abandon the app, so you'll want to push them to take the next step by encouraging or even incentivizing them to do so.

In-App Messaging

As users onboard your app, you'll want to engage them with in-app messages, also known as in-app notifications. As the name implies, these are messages sent to your users while they are active in your mobile app. They tend to give reminders of relevant information, but don't always call for immediate action:

- Ask the user to rate the app experience.
- Announce version upgrades or new features.
- Request access to a user's location or phone contacts to enable key app features.
- Provide tool tips surrounding key features. Tool tips are small, interactive pop-up boxes that appear when a user hovers over, clicks on, or focuses on an element in an app.

With the new app learning curve ever looming, in-app messages work to increase product usage while making feature discoverability and usage that much easier.

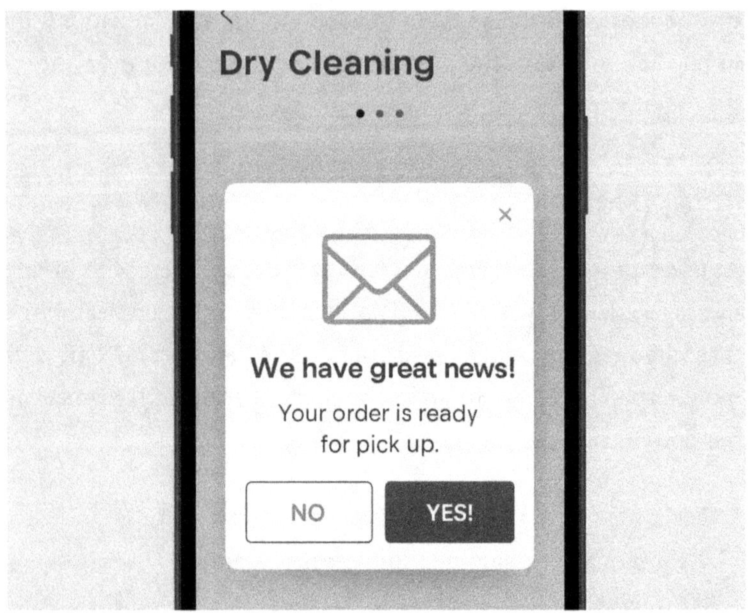

Push Notifications

Similar to in-app messages, push notifications are messages sent directly to the user. While the former communicates with people currently using the application, the latter sends messages outside the app to get the attention of users who don't currently have it open.

The two most common types of push notifications you'll see include *rich media*, when a link or content is provided alongside the message, and *geo-pushes*, where the message is tied to your location. Many founders use push notifications to individualize their app experience and give it a more personalized feel. Since they're completely customizable, the possibilities are endless. For example, let's say you were to book a trip through a travel app. A few days later, you receive a push notification reminding you of your travel date and time. This will likely prompt you to open the app to see additional information about travel requirements or even flight changes. Push notifications can be applied to specific actions like using particular features, making a purchase, or bookmarking items as favorites.

Route users back to your app with push notifications.

App users who receive one or more notifications in their first 90 days have an average retention rate nearly 3x higher than users who receive no push notifications.[3]

Remarketing and Retargeting

Now I know I've been advocating pretty hard for the benefits of app messaging, but there is a catch: Over 40 percent of users opt out of push notifications.[4] Many people don't like being bothered with extra notifications, even if those messages can benefit them. You've probably opted out of a few yourself.

A popular way of mitigating the opt-out of push notifications is through *remarketing* and *retargeting*. These terms are often used interchangeably, but they entail different methods of reengaging users who have interacted with your app. Remarketing focuses more on content, such as email campaigns, to reach out to users and bring them back to the app. Retargeting, on the other hand, uses cookies and tracking *pixels* to reengage users through paid ads on various platforms.

Tracking pixels are small, invisible images embedded in emails or web pages that track user behavior by sending information back to a server when the pixel is triggered. To integrate tracking pixels into your app, you typically add the pixel code provided by a service like Facebook or Google into your app's code base—usually in the header section—allowing you to monitor user interactions and tailor your marketing strategies accordingly.

Have you ever visited an app and then seen ads for that same app on other websites for the next few days? Yep, you've been retargeted.

Retention Best Practices

Whether you're using one or all the tactics listed previously, there are few practices to keep in mind to ensure things go smoothly.

Don't Overpromise

Nobody goes into building an app with the hopes of delivering a lackluster product, but sometimes it takes time to build and grow an app that's up to par. It is possible to attract and maintain a user following in the meantime, but you must be realistic and transparent about the progress of the product along the way.

That starts with managing expectations and setting healthy boundaries around what you can practically deliver and in what timeframe. For example, telling your users that you can fix a bug in two days when it will take your development at least three weeks not only puts unnecessary pressure on your team but also creates a sense of mistrust and dishonesty around your company. Users can learn to be patient, but they won't be so willing to trust a founder who doesn't keep their word.

Ask for Feedback

Continually seek new ways to collect feedback both in and off the app. As a founder, it can be hard to humble yourself to ask for others' insights, especially when you know some responses will be less than positive. You must learn to remove your ego from the process.

I've wanted to clap back at unreasonable user comments more times than I'd like to admit, but I grew to realize that it isn't personal. Most people simply want to be acknowledged and know their issue isn't going unnoticed.

Ultimately, a user's lack of understanding, confusion, or poor experience *is* your responsibility—but that is not necessarily a reflection of the hard work or dedication you've put into building your app. Feedback is just an opportunity to get better.

Track Metrics

When it comes to apps—if it wasn't measured, it didn't happen.

You can't set benchmarks for future success if you don't know where you're currently at. Set campaign and monthly goals with your team, and take the time weekly to review your performance with some of the following metrics:

- *Daily active users (DAUs):* How many users open the app daily?
- *Session length:* How long does a user interact with the pages in your app?
- *Time in-app:* How much time does a user spend in your app overall from day to day (the culmination of all their sessions combined)?
- *Churn rate:* At what rate do users offload your app?
- *Cost per acquisition:* How much does it cost you to acquire a customer? If you're using paid marketing tactics, be mindful that you will likely also need to dedicate costs toward retaining them.

APPRENEUR INSIGHT

"Incremental iteration has had limited benefit on my journeys for product-market fit. More success comes from clear go and no-go minimums and having those revolve around major shifts in metrics. You should have a ruthless focus on major metric movement."[5]

~Dan Kihanya, Director REI Path Ahead Ventures, Creator of Founders Unfound podcast

Ultimately, I believe the key to mastering user retention is finding the delicate balance between delivering on what users tell you they want through feedback and giving them what you believe they need based on what the data supports.

Maintenance

As we close out this chapter, let's briefly dive into creating a maintenance and management cadence for your app.

APPRENEUR INSIGHT

One thing you don't realize is that products always need maintenance and testing. Novice founders get excited when a product is delivered to them, then are surprised months down the road when the product's performance decreases as users begin to accumulate and engagement increases. One of the biggest mistakes is misunderstanding MVP vs. V 1.0. MVP is to validate that the problem you're solving for does exist and users see value in your product to help them solve this problem. MVP is not intended to exist as your commercial product that you intend to scale with. V 1.0 is for scale, and it will require more advanced development. The best case is that your development team has built your MVP to scale with your business, so it can be enhanced to serve as your V 1.0. Sometimes you may have to jettison your MVP and start from scratch, but this should only be the case if your MVP convicted you through data and customer feedback to pivot to a different product or approach.[6]

~Chris Davis, CEO at Fansub

I've provided a brief overview of app maintenance to give you some insights and context into what to anticipate, how often you should be updating your app, and the support you'll need to streamline this process to make it a part of your regular routine.

What Maintenance Insights Should I Track?

When you start entertaining the idea of updating your app, it's natural to assume those updates will be focused on adding new bells and whistles. But the reality is a lot more practical. There are a variety of reasons you might be required to update your app, and you'll need to be prepared for them all to maintain a presence in the app stores. A few of the more common reasons are listed here:

- *New device releases:* New devices often come with new size dimensions that your app will be required to adjust to.
- *Platform updates:* App stores often have policy and performance updates that all developers must adhere to.
- *Programming language updates:* Code can get outdated; be sure your product isn't lagging behind because you failed to address an update.
- *User demands:* Occasionally, you'll need to tweak a product based on user feedback. This may not always be an enhancement; it's often a correction to make sure the app works as intended.
- *Security standards:* Protecting your users and your company should be a top priority. Make it your mission to protect data and stay on top of legal guidelines to ensure everyone is safe and within policy.

You should anticipate emails from the app stores announcing upcoming changes. Most updates and announcements come weeks to months in advance, so you likely won't find yourself blindsided, but you still need to be prepared.

Strive to make updates a part of your cadence, not a distraction from it. Meet with your team early to establish a recurring rhythm for when you will assess analytics, data reports, and feedback and begin to create sprints around quality assurance and ongoing improvements.

How Often Should I Update My App?

Update your app as often as you can afford to or as much as you need to. Will there be a change to make every day? Probably not. But there will likely be subtle enhancements you can make weekly to monthly to ensure you're staying on top of your game.

Currently, many free apps are updated every eighteen days, while paid apps are updated around every fifty-three days.[7]

Who Should Be Maintaining My App?

The obvious answer to the question of who should be maintaining your app is whoever built your app. Many development agencies offer complimentary maintenance for the first three to six months after deployment, followed by retainer packages thereafter.

If your developer or agency does not provide these services, you can hire a freelancer to do work à la carte or hourly as issues arise. You can also leverage another firm to do ongoing maintenance, as it never hurts to have a go-to team on standby.

What Are the Costs Associated with Updating My App?

As you think about the post-deployment phase of your app, please keep your budget in mind. There is an assortment of costs associated with maintaining an app, and you want to include those in your operational plans. Some of these costs include the following:

- *Maintenance team:* As mentioned in the previous section, if you're not technical, you'll need someone to make updates to your app. Retainers give you responsiveness on-demand, but à la carte or hourly support can be more budget-friendly.
- *Hosting and servers: I*deally, your app is going to grow in data, sales, and usership, and when those milestones reach a certain point you may need to scale your servers. Unless you experience explosive growth really quickly, the hosting your developers start you with should be sufficient for some time, but if you do grow, be prepared to pay more for these services. Note: Moving forward, you may hear the terms *hosting* and *server* used interchangeably, but they refer to related yet distinct aspects of web infrastructure. Hosting is a service provided by hosting companies and involves the allocation of space on a server for storing your app.
- *Software and solutions:* As you get in sync, you'll need to think about the recurring cost of the SaaS (software-as-a-service) tools you'll need to operate the business and maintain data and insights, and ancillary services you need to improve user experience. These may include but aren't limited to the following:
    - Crash analytics and monitoring

- Push notifications services
- Mobile engagement platform

When it comes to apps, the work isn't endless, but it is ongoing. Stay diligent and consistent to ensure you can preserve your business and keep giving your users the best experience possible for as long as possible. You've made it all the way here—you owe it to yourself and your customers to protect your investment.

Chapter checklist

- [ ] Devise a retention strategy for your app.
- [ ] Consult with your development team to outline a maintenance plan.

AFTERWORD

Welcome to App Entrepreneurship

The decision to learn how to build apps changed my life and expanded my world.

Never could I have imagined that these little bundles of software would enrich me in the way they have.

I have learned that I am capable of doing hard things. That I love myself enough to show up for me and my ideas, even when they seem out of reach. That with a bit of discipline, consistency, and faith, I can do all things.

This journey has taken me to literal heights, like visiting the mountains of Uludağ, Turkey, to speak about my products, and has grounded me with gratitude during chance encounters with strangers who use my apps. From wedding invites from our dating app users to being flown to the Caribbean to offer a consultation, I am in awe of what one decision has led to and am continually humbled by life's generosity.

And yet despite what it looks like now, none of it has been easy. Even today, with years of skin in the game, I still wouldn't describe the work as effortless. There have been seasons of confusion, financial strain, disappointment, and back-to-back letdowns. What you see now is a reflection of years of pure grind—month after month of doing the work that most people wouldn't and a healthy disregard for the impossible. It is a reflection of putting myself out there even when I was embarrassed and sticking to it even though I was scared.

This book is a testament to the notion that with practice, difficult things become doable.

I say this to make clear that what you put into this book is what you will get out of it. If you take shortcuts, skip the assignments, and find yourself repeatedly saying, *"I don't think I need to do that,"* the sum of your decisions will be reflected in your product. If this process has taught me nothing else, it's that you simply can't outrun the work.

Building my first app was a lonely and costly process, and it is my sincere hope that with the assistance of this book, the experience will be different for you. I have poured my heart into these pages in an attempt to offer you insights, but more importantly, a community. Appreneurship does not have to be an island. You now belong to a cohort of fellow creators. A village of dreamers who may share inexperience but make up for it in motivation. Your tribe awaits.

I invite you to join The App Accelerator, the world's most comprehensive and robust community for tech-challenged entrepreneurs. Our community empowers aspiring appreneurs like you to develop, fund, market, launch, and scale their app ideas, generating recurring income within a year—all without wasting time or money—even if they have no technical skills.

Unlock a treasure trove of tools and resources beyond these pages by signing up. Gain access to a foundry of invaluable resources, including the following:

- *Chapter-themed video tutorials and expanded guides:* Get more out of every chapter with interactive video walk-throughs and bonus educational resources.
- *Developer directory:* Match-make with the right technical team to bring your idea to life using our curated list of proven agencies.
- *App creation toolbox:* Cut through the clutter with this list of recommended and industry-renowned tools, including AI-powered resources like No Code Captain and App Cost Estimator.
- *Exclusive interviews with leading app and mobile experts:* Gain insider insights from some of the world's leading app professionals.
- *Tech tutorials and training:* Skip the learning curve with our comprehensive mini tech tutorials, video walk-throughs, and trainings on essential tools and techniques.
- *Activities, tutorials, and worksheets:* Download and print activities, charts, and worksheets from our success library of solutions.
- *Sample documents and contract templates:* Get a head start with our templates for essential business documents and contracts.
- *Investment readiness toolkit:* Equip yourself with tools, resources, and education to develop your cap table, create a robust data room, and enhance your appeal to investors.
- *App coaching support services:* Access our team of experienced app advisors and participate in monthly coaching huddles for personalized guidance and feedback.

And more!

Visit IHaveAnAppIdea.net or TheAppAccelerator.com to sign up today.

Thank you for entrusting me as your guide. I can't wait to see what you create. You're up next, appreneur!

Notes

INTRODUCTION PREPARE TO BUILD

1. Robert F. Smith, LinkedIn post, December 16, 2024, https://www.linkedin.com/feed/update/urn:li:activity:7274458726349037570/.

2. Steve Jobs, "Steve Jobs Secrets of Life," interview by John McLaughlin, November 11, 1994, "Steve Jobs 1994 Interview," 0:35 to 0:52, https://youtu.be/kYfNvmF0Bqw.

CHAPTER 1: BEFORE YOU BEGIN

1. Stan Burenko, "How Long Does It Take to Make an App?," *UpTech*, April 5, 2022, https://www.uptech.team/blog/how-long-does-it-take-to-make-an-app.

2. Nichole Yembra, interview by author, December 12, 2022. Transcript available on Formly.

3. McKeever "Mac" Conwell II, interview by author, September 20, 2022. Transcript available on Formly.

4. George Deeb, "Is Your Startup Building a 'Vitamin' or a 'Painkiller'?," *Forbes, July 24, 2014, https://www.forbes.com/sites/georgedeeb/2014/07/24/is-your-startup-building-a-vitamin-or-a-painkiller/.*

5. Barney Spann, interview by author, August 20, 2023. Transcript available on Formly.

CHAPTER 2 DEVELOPING A WINNING START-UP IDEA

1. Eric Reis, "Minimum Viable Product: A Guide," *Startup Lessons Learned (blog), August 3, 2009, https://www.startuplessonslearned.com/2009/08/minimum-viable-product-guide.html.*

2. Meredith Hart, "16 Examples of Positioning Statements & How to Craft Your Own," *HubSpot (blog), HubSpot.com, June 20,2023.*

3. Gail Brooks, Alan Heffner, and Dave Henderson, "A SWOT Analysis of Competitive Knowledge from Social Media for a Small Start-Up Business," *Review of Business Information Systems (RBIS) 18, no. 1 (2014), https://doi.org/10.19030/rbis.v18i1.8540.*

4. Nneka Ukpai, interview by author, October 29, 2023. Transcript available on Formly.

5. Yembra, interview.

6. Clayton M Christensen, Mark W Johnson, and Darrell K Rigby, "Foundations for Growth: How to Identify and Build Disruptive New Businesses," *MIT Sloan Management Review (2002).*

7. Eric Sonnier, interview by author, December 13, 2022. Transcript available on Formly.

8. "A Playbook for Achieving Product-Market Fit," Lean Startup Co. Education Program, https://leanstartup.co/resources/articles/a-playbook-for-achieving-product-market-fit/.

9.Eric Ries, *The Lean Startup: How Today's Entrepreneurs Use Continuous Innovation to Create Radically Successful Businesses (Crown Business, 2011).*

10. Anders Toxboe, "Product Experiment: Fake Door Testing," *Learning Loop, January 10, 2019, https://learningloop.io/plays/fake-door-testing.*

11. Gijs van Wulfen, "Experiment with Innovation Like Tesla," LinkedIn.com, October 10, 2016, https://finance.yahoo.com/news/experiment-innovation-tesla-102635081.html.

12. Matthew Hall, interview by author, August 21, 2023. Transcript available on Formly.

CHAPTER 4 THE BUSINESS OF APPS

1. Daniel Howley, "Apple says it's paid out $320 billion to developers since 2008 as App Store fight heats up," Yahoo Finance, January 10, 2023, https://finance.yahoo.com/news/apple-says-its-paid-out-320-billion-to-developers-since-2008-as-app-store-fight-heats-up-191521817.html.

2. Apple Developer, "Enrolling, verifying, and renewing with the Apple Developer app,"

https://developer.apple.com/support/app-account/.

3. Avinash Sharma, "How to Upload an App to Google Play Store?," *Appinventiv* (blog), June 13, 2023, https://appinventiv.com/blog/how-to-submit-app-to-google-play-store/.

4. Ian Carlos Campbell and Julia Alexander, "A Guide to Platform Fees," *The Verge, August 24, 2021, https://www.theverge.com/21445923/platform-fees-apps-games-business-marketplace-apple-google.*

5. Paolo Roma and Daniele Ragaglia, "Revenue Models, in-App Purchase, and the App Performance: Evidence from Apple's App Store and Google Play," *Electronic Commerce Research and Applications 17 (2016): 173–90, https://doi.org/10.1016/j.elerap.2016.04.007.*

6. Predicts 2014: Mobile and Wireless, Gartner, 2014.

7. Luciana Brito, "Portraits of Black Politics and Resistance in Brazil," Nacla.org, June 17, 2022, https://nacla.org/black-politics-resistance-brazil.

CHAPTER 5 APP ABC'S: DESIGN AND DEVELOPMENT

1. R. Dinakar, "Types of Mobile Apps: Native, Hybrid, Web and Progressive Web Apps," *PCloudy (blog), May 30, 2023, https://www.pcloudy.com/blogs/types-of-mobile-apps-native-hybrid-web-and-progressive-web-apps/.*

2. William Jobe, "Native Apps vs. Mobile Web Apps," *International Journal of Interactive Mobile Technologies 7, no. 4 (2013), https://doi.org/10.3991/ijim.v7i4.3226.*

3. Minh Q. Huynh, Prashant Ghimire, and Donny Truong, "Hybrid App Approach: Could It Mark the End of Native App Domination?," *Issues in Informing Science and Information Technology 14 (2017): 049–65, https://doi.org/10.28945/3723.*

CHAPTER 6 YOUR DEVELOPMENT OPTIONS: CHOOSING THE BEST PATH FOR YOU

1. Yonghui Liu, Xiao Chen, Yue Liu, Pingfan Kong, Tegawendé F Bissyande, Jacques Klein, Xiaoyu Sun, Chunyang Chen, and John Grundy, *A Comparative Study of Smartphone and Smart Tv Apps (Elsevier, 2022).*

2. "KweliTV," Kweli.tv, August 22, 2022.

3. Kevin Borgolte and Nick Feamster, "Understanding the Performance Costs and Benefits of Privacy-Focused Browser Extensions," paper presented at the Proceedings of The Web Conference, 2020.

4. Jack Flynn, "Wordpress Market Share+ Statistics[2023]: How many websites use Wordpress?," Zippia.com, February 6, 2023.

CHAPTER 7 DESIGNING YOUR APP

1. Jermaine Henry, interview by author, September 1, 2022. Transcript available on Formly.

2. Sonnier, interview.

3. Ina Fried, "One in Four Mobile Apps Are Abandoned After a Single Use," Vox.com, June 13, 2015, https://www.vox.com/2015/6/13/11563532/one-in-four-mobile-apps-are-abandoned-after-a-single-use.

1. Suzanne Robertson and James Robertson, *Mastering the Requirements Process: Getting Requirements Right (Addison-Wesley, 2012).*

2. Dan Kihanya, interview by author, August 7, 2022. Transcript available on Formly.

3. "What Is MoSCoW Prioritization?," *ProductPlan (blog), https://www.productplan.com/glossary/moscow-prioritization/.*

4. Jermaine Henry, interview by author, September 1, 2022. Transcript available on Formly.

5. Spann, interview.

CHAPTER 9 BUILDING YOUR DEV TEAM

1. Sonnier, interview.

2. Yembra, interview.

3. Davis, interview.

4. Spann, interview.

CHAPTER 10 ONBOARDING YOUR DEVELOPMENT AGENCY

1. David Pawlan, interview by author, August 5, 2022. Transcript available on Formly.

2. Ukpai, interview.

3. Chris Davis, interview by author, September 14, 2023. Transcript available on Formly.

4. Michael Meng, Stephanie Steinhardt, and Andreas Schubert, "Application Programming Interface Documentation: What Do Software Developers Want?," *Journal of Technical Writing and Communication 48, no. 3 (2018): 295–330,* https://doi.org/10.1177/0047281617721853.

5. T. Bhuvaneswari and S. Prabaharan, "A Survey on Software Development Life Cycle Models," *International Journal of Computer Science and Mobile Computing 2, no. 5 (2013): 262–67.*

6. John Erickson, Kalle Lyytinen, and Keng Siau, "Agile Modeling, Agile Software Development, and Extreme Programming: The State of Research," *Journal of Database Management (JDM) 16, no. 4 (2005): 88–100.*

7. Faisal Hayat, Ammar Ur Rehman, Khawaja Sarmad Arif, Kanwal Wahab, and Muhammad Abbas, "The Influence of Agile Methodology (Scrum) on Software Project Management," in *2019 20th IEEE/ACIS International Conference on Software Engineering, Artificial Intelligence, Networking and Parallel/Distributed Computing (SNPD)* (IEEE/ACIS, 2019), 145–49.

8. Paul Klipp, "Getting Started with Kanban," *Amazon Digital Services, 2014.*

9. Pawlan, interview.

CHAPTER 11 CREATING YOUR APP'S ASSETS

1. Jasmine Shells, interview by author, August 31, 2022. Transcript available on Formly.

2. "Brand & marketing resources," Developer.android.com, August 23, 2023, https://developer.android.com/distribute/marketing-tools.

3. Hall, interview.

CHAPTER 12 TESTING YOUR APP

1. Shells, interview.

1. Programs.Developer.Apple.com, August 23,2023, https://developer.apple.com/programs/.

2. Ibid.

3. "App Store Review Guidelines," Developer.Apple.com, August 23, 2023,

https://developer.apple.com/app-store/review/guidelines/.

4. "Guideline 2.3.3—Performance—Accurate Metadata," *Apple Developer Forums, accessed July 17, 2023, https://developer.apple.com/forums/thread/95851.*

5. "Guideline 5.1—Legal—Privacy—Data Collection and Storage," *Apple Developer Forums, accessed July 17, 2023, https://developer.apple.com/forums/thread/656591.*

6. "Guideline 4.1—Design—Copycats (Please Demonstrate Your Relationship with Any Third-Party Brand Owners Represented in Your App.)," *Apple Developer Forums, accessed July 17, 2023, https://developer.apple.com/forums/thread/85002.*

7. Anna Heim, "Apple's App Store Connect will be open on Christmas: Can developers take advantage?" TechCrunch.com, *December 22, 2021, https://techcrunch.com/2021/12/22/apples-app-store-connect-will-be-open-on-christmas-can-developers-take-advantage/.*

8. "What is an EULA and how to generate one?," Iubenda.com, September 15, 2023, https://www.iubenda.com/en/help/22363-what-is-an eula#:~:text=In%20fact%2C%20as%20mentioned%20before,you%20and%20the%20end%20user.

9. "Number of apps available in leading app stores as of 3rd quarter 2022, Statista.com, September 15, 2023, https://www.statista.com/statistics/276623/number-of-apps-available-in-leading-app-stores/.

10."Google Play Developer Distribution Agreement," Google Play, September 15, 2023, https://play.google.com/intl/en_us/about/developer-distribution-agreement.html.

11. "Developer Policy Center," Google Play, September 15, 2023, https://play.google.com/about/developer-content-policy/.

12. "International Age Rating Coalition," Global Ratings, September 15, 2023, https://www.globalratings.com/about.aspx.

13. "APK Expansion Files," developer.android.com, September 15, 2023. https://developer.android.com/google/play/expansion-files.

CHAPTER 14 ENGAGING AND ATTRACTING USERS

1. Scott D. Clary, "How Tinder Acquired 50 Million Users," Hackernoon.com, July 1, 2021, https://hackernoon.com/how-tinder-acquired-50-million-users-z1o35nw.

2. Conwell II, interview.

3. Adam L. Penenberg, *Viral loop: From Facebook to Twitter, How Today's Smartest Businesses Grow Themselves (Hachette Books), 2009.*

4. Abdul Wahab,"How Robinhood Did a Stellar Pre-Launch Campaign," *Prefinery* (blog), March 14, 2023. https://www.prefinery.com/blog/referral-programs prelaunch-campaign/robinhood/.

5. Rochelle King, Elizabeth F. Churchill, and Caitlin Tan, *Designing with Data: Improving the User Experience with A/B Testing (O'Reilly Media, 2017).*

6. Rebecca Lieb, Content Marketing: Think Like a Publisher—How to Use Content to Market Online and In Social Media (Que Publishing, 2012).

7. Diederich Bakker, "Conceptualising Influencer Marketing," *Journal of Emerging Trends in Marketing and Management 1, no. 1 (2018): 79–87.*

CHAPTER 15 MAINTAINING MOMENTUM: RETENTION AND APP UPKEEP

1. "4 methods to boost mobile app user retention in 2024," *Zendrive* (blog), October 27, 2024. https://www.zendrive.com/blog/mobile-app-user-retention#:~:-text=According%20to%20a%20Business%20of,days%20after%20installing%20the%20app. "

2. "21% of Users Abandon an App After One Use," UplandSoftware.com, 2018,

https://uplandsoftware.com/localytics/resources/blog/21-percent-of-users-abandon-apps-after-one-use/.

3. "How Push Notifications Impact Mobile App Retention Rates," Urban Airship.com, 2017, chrome-extension://efaidnbmnnnibpcajpcglclefindmkaj/https://grow.urbanairship.com/rs/313-QPJ-195/images/WP_App_Retention_Rates_Benchmarks.pdf.

4. "30+ Push Notification Statistics (New 2025 Data)," wisernotify.com, 2025, https://wisernotify.com/blog/push-notification-stats/.

5. Kihanya, interview.

6. Davis, interview.

7. Nadine Mansour, "How Often Should You Update Your Paid Mobile App?," Instabug.com, October 31, 2019, https://www.instabug.com/blog/how-often-should-you-update-your-paid-mobile-app.

www.ingramcontent.com/pod-product-compliance
Lightning Source LLC
LaVergne TN
LVHW020707110826
845149LV00012B/2149

9781964686578